OWNER'S GUIDE TO SEWING MACHINES, SERGERS, AND KNITTING MACHINES

Other books in the Creative Machine Arts Series, available from Chilton:

OWNER'S GUIDE TO SEWING MACHINES, SERGERS, AND KNITTING MACHINES

GALE GRIGG HAZEN

Chilton Book Company
Radnor, Pennsylvania

Designed by Anthony Jacobson
Illustrations by Pam Poole
Cover artwork by Margaret Cusack
Cover photograph by Larry Brazil
Manufactured in the United States of America

Library of Congress Cataloging in Publication Data

Hazen, Gale Grigg.
    Owner's guide to sewing machines, sergers, and knitting machines
  Gale Grigg Hazen.
        p.   cm.—(Creative machine arts)
    Includes index.
    ISBN 0-8019-7888-2
    1. Machine sewing.   2. Sewing machines—Maintenance and repair.
  3. Knitting, Machine.   4. Knitting-machines—Maintenance and repair.
  I. Title.   II. Series: Creative machine arts series.
  TT713.H38   1989
  646.2'044—dc20
                                                        88-43310
                                                            CIP

1 2 3 4 5 6 7 8 9 0   8 7 6 5 4 3 2 1 0 9

CONTENTS

FOREWORD

Inside me is a certain level of mechanical ignorance that I detest. Somehow I missed the general science classes that would have made me familiar with the concepts of, say, electricity, so that when the switch on the lamp in the living room broke, I would easily dive inside it for a look-see. Instead, the lamp's been sitting there dark for months, causing me great inconvenience.

Ah-ha! I will invite Gale Hazen to my house. She has the kind of inquiring mind that's unafraid of electricity. Undoubtedly, she will whip out a screwdriver from her purse and dismantle the switch, all the while muttering, "I wonder why *this thing won't work."*

And that same attitude is why you will enjoy Gale's book: she helps you understand why *your sewing machine, serger, and knitting machine do and do not work. Better yet, she will encourage your curiosity about the mechanical workings of your beloved machines. You, too, will want to whip out a screwdriver and look inside. Suddenly, you will understand why cheap thread breaks; why the unconventional use of the embroidery presser foot can prevent ruffling on sweater knit seams; why you should not use metal tweezers to dig around in the bobbin case; why you should never put plastic covers on your machines; why a serger needs to be oiled and used often.*

Gale's approach is funny—I can't wait to teach my daughter one of Gale's rules: don't spit into your machine—yet she also gives you the courage to explore your machines. In fact, after I took one of her serger classes, in which we practically dismantled and rebuilt it, I felt so bold that when I came home, I completely took apart my coffee grinder and cleaned it for the first time in five years.

Now you, too, can invite Gale into your home through this book. May she turn on the light for all of us.

Robbie Fanning

Editor, Creative Machine Arts, and
co-author, *The Complete Book of Machine Embroidery*

PREFACE

Do you ever feel that the main obstacle between you and your beautifully made garment or craft is your sewing machine? If you often have the urge to throw your machine through the nearest window, take heart: There *is* rhyme and reason to how that piece of mechanical frustration can be helped to work its best.

Sewing is an art, not a science. As such, there are no absolute answers as to why problems occur and no one-shot formulas for solving them. Each project involves different variables of fabric, thread, needles, presser feet, etc., so each sewing session must be analyzed with *all* these elements in mind.

As an avid home sewer and a sewing instructor, I had encountered the frustration of puckers, skipped stitches, broken threads, and jams more than once. When I began sewing machine repair training and understood how the machine functioned, the causes behind these problems soon became clear. I realized all home sewers need a good basic knowledge of the sewing machine itself to make sewing easier and more enjoyable.

In this book you will not find "easy-reference" or "troubleshooting" charts, because I am convinced they don't truly teach you to understand why your machine may not be working the way you want. My intent is to present the information that will allow you to make reasonable, intelligent choices based on an understanding of the interrelationships between your machine and the variables you bring to it. I also want to dispel misconceptions about how sewing machines function and give you hints on breaking bad habits, especially unconscious ones. I will help you build the foundation that you can continue to strengthen forever.

The book is organized in layers, each chapter building on the last. *Because the order in which the information is presented is critical to your understanding, kindly read the part on your machine straight through the first time.* (Don't use the index until you have read the entire section on your sewing or knitting machine or serger. Read all the information, not just the parts you might think you need help with.) The information may seem quite new; don't worry if it isn't all crystal clear immediately. You might need to read certain sections more than once. But please wade on through the first time; you will be fine.

A sewing machine or serger is like a Chinese puzzle box: all the pieces must work in sequence before the puzzle can be solved. Likewise, it is important to understand the *entire* chain in the sewing process—the layers—so that you can chip away at the problems yourself, one step at a time. This book is therefore not so much for the times when everything is working perfectly, but for when it is not.

This book is not a technical repair manual, because that's beyond the scope of my intention. But I distill the essence of that knowledge here to give every level of home sewer practical tools to solve "operator-caused" problems. The perspective I offer is different from other books because of my training in repair of all kinds of sewing machines, plus three decades of sewing.

The book came about in answer to a void I discovered in the basic knowledge of most home sewers; they couldn't relate their sewing troubles to how the machine functioned and therefore were dependent on an industry that rarely supplied correct or sufficient information to the public. I found that, for example, many sewers would automatically reach for "the tension" when something went wrong, not realizing that knob or dial is rarely the real source of the problems.

My heart goes out to all the people who are flooded with misinformation that makes them hate sewing—or worse yet, who have quit because of frustration with their machines. My hope is to help you become good friends with your machine so that you might bring out your best talents and ideas while discovering the joys that creating your own garments and crafts can bring.

If I succeed in changing your approach to sewing, then this book will have served its purpose and will remain by your machine as a reference.

Gale Grigg Hazen

ACKNOWLEDGMENTS

Many people have contributed to the experiences that made this book possible. I would like to thank a few in particular:

The students and customers who asked the questions so that I could learn what needed to be answered;

Ed, with whom I apprenticed to learn about repairing sewing machines;

all the other reps and teaching technicians who aided the learning process;

Beth Witrogen McLeod, for helping me to write, teaching me to write, and encouraging me to write on my own;

my friends and associates, for all their support and encouragement over the years, in believing that my class should be turned into book form;

last but not least, my husband Dennis and daughters Gena and Cara, for putting up with me while doing this book.

PART I
SEWING MACHINES

RULES OF READING

Before we begin, I first want you to read the manual that came with your sewing machine. If you have lost or misplaced it, buy or borrow another. Read it as you would a novel. Then reread it every year. Make a date, such as April Fool's or your birthday, to help you remember. In this way the knowledge of how your machine is set up will remain fresh.

As you read, please note where the following items are positioned on your machine so that you will recognize them by name as they appear later. Whereas all machines feature these parts, they may be located in slightly different areas, look different, or have different names. Look at the drawing or photo in your manual. Better yet, photocopy it and attach it to this page.

1. Handwheel
2. Take-up lever
3. Upper tension mechanism
4. Stitch selector (pattern)
5. Stitch width selector
6. Stitch length selector
7. Feed dogs
8. Throat plate and hole
9. Bobbin casing*
10. Lower tension screw
11. Presser foot lifter
12. Needle
13. Needle clamp screw
14. Bobbin winder

15. Power switch
16. Pressure regulator*

*not available on all machines

There are also other parts they never told you about, such as the race, shuttle, hook, and separating plates.

Before you begin working on the machine, please check your power cord. The cord can actually disintegrate over time and cause fires. When I worked in the repair shop, I was constantly amazed by how many machines had cords with exposed wires. Check your manual to learn if your machine shuts off power to the cord when the light is off. Some electric circuits are broken only when the cord itself is unplugged. This can be a safety hazard, according to *Consumer Reports,* so unplug the machine each time you finish sewing.

▶ Unplug the cord by holding the plug. Never yank it out of the socket by the cord.

1

HOW A SEWING MACHINE REALLY WORKS

I once had a student who came to me in class and said, "I'm having problems with my machine. It breaks threads when I start to sew." I suggested that maybe she was turning the handwheel backward to remove the needle from the fabric. She said, "Absolutely not. I never, ever do that!" The next week she came in and said, "I still don't think I did that, but since you told me, I haven't broken any threads."

That is the best example I can give to explain what I believe causes the majority of home-sewing frustrations: what I call mind-set. We aren't always aware of our unconscious habits. Our mind-set is what causes them.

We all work from a basic knowledge at whatever we do. Much of it is habit, or unconscious. Once we establish a mind-set on false information, however, we have no firm base on which to build real understanding. It's like trying to create a recipe using the wrong ingredients: nothing works and you don't know why. That is why mind-sets can be dangerous. They prevent us from discovering the true source of our problems.

For example, the first time we learned to sew, we visualized how the stitch was formed by using a needle and thread and making the stitch by hand. Then came the sewing machine. We still maintained an image of how it functioned from our earlier experience. When it didn't work this way, it became the antagonist and sewing became a frustrating experience.

To think of a machine's functioning in terms of hand sewing is the single most erroneous mind-set we can have. To understand how the machine makes a stitch, and to introduce the foundation of the book, I want you to sit down at your sewing machine and perform the only exercise I will ask of you. The reason for the exercise will become clear as you read on.

Thread the needle and bobbin with a light color thread, as if you are about to begin sewing. Take a felt-tip pen and mark the upper thread about five inches above the eye of the needle. Slowly sew a scrap of material at straight stitch and watch what happens to the mark. You will see that it slides repeatedly through the eye, up and down—about 40 to 60

Fig. 1.1

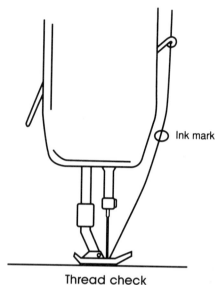

Ink mark

Thread check

times, depending on the stitch length—before it is actually sewn into the fabric (Fig. 1.1).

The needle moves all the way down to its lowest point. As it comes back up again, the fabric closes around it. If you could see inside the machine, you would see a bubble or loop of thread forming as the needle rises (Fig. 1.2). The hook then comes past and spreads the thread over the bobbin casing to form the knot that holds the fabric together. That's why when you try to remove your fabric from the sewing machine, sometimes it doesn't pull out freely. The needle is out, but the thread is still

Fig. 1.2

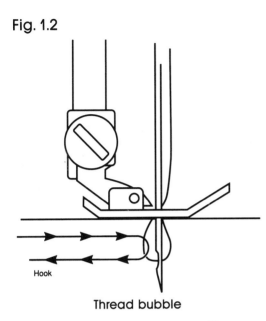

Hook

Thread bubble

wrapped around the bobbin. The stitch is finished and the fabric will always pull out easily when the uptake is at its uppermost point.

Upper Threading

To understand how the machine functions, we will trace the process by which the thread travels through it, encounters resistance or tension, and ends by making stitches to create your garments or crafts.

The Escapements

The spool of thread sits on a spool holder. Whether the spindle is horizontal or vertical has relatively little to do with stitch quality.

After the thread leaves the spool, it travels through an "escapement"— meaning that it passes through and escapes out again. All escapements put some measure of resistance or drag against the thread, a pull measured in tiny increments called gram weights.

Because a machine is set up according to gram weights, and since each escapement adds its portion of resistance to the total pull, it is critical to thread the machine through each one, without exception. If you miss even one, either intentionally or accidentally, you can throw off the tension and your stitches won't form correctly.

Contrary to belief, tension is not that little adjustable knob or dial on the front of the machine. **Tension is the resistance against the thread as it travels through the machine.** It is the interrelationship of all the layers that combines to form a stitch: thread, needle, presser foot, fabric.

The next escapement the thread travels through is what I will hereafter refer to as the upper "tension mechanism" or "tension assembly," that knob or dial with the numbers or "plus and minus" indicators.

▶ Your best rule of thumb is the higher the number or greater degree of "plus," the tighter the tension, and vice versa.

The Separating Disks: The Tension Assembly

Inside the tension assembly, the thread will pass through shiny separating plates or disks. Refer to your manual if you aren't sure of the proper direction for threading. If you are using two threads, check for an extra center. Make sure the threads pass on either side of the disk, if your machine features that option. These metal pieces are what press together and hold onto the thread with more or less firmness, depending on the mechanism's setting. Only when the presser foot lifter is completely lowered do these disks come together and engage the tension on the thread (Fig. 1.3).

▶ There are no best settings for all tension assemblies. Each machine is set up by a mechanic and tension depends on many factors, including his or her skill. The same amount of tension, or gram weight of pull, could therefore be achieved on the

Fig. 1.3

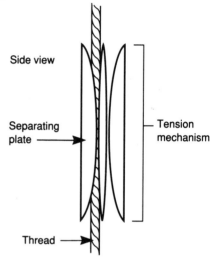

Side view

Separating plate

Tension mechanism

Thread

Separating plate squeezes against thread

same brand machine at "3" or at "5". It depends on an internal setting, which can always be readjusted by a mechanic.

The separating plates hold the thread taut by means of a spring. One of the major differences in machines is in the quality of that spring. It can be a single-action spring that holds the thread, or it can be geared, so that it holds more securely and consistently with a thicker, more durable spring made of stronger metal.

The advantage of a geared spring is that you can change the amount of stress by finer, more exact degrees. This allows for a greater degree of control and more frequent adjustments without fear of wearing out or slipping, or compressing, the spring.

▶ If your machine was manufactured more than twenty-five years ago, you may have been advised to leave the presser foot lifter down when you aren't sewing. That was because the spring was not as sturdy as those made today. Leaving the spring in continual contraction eventually compresses it permanently, which affects the tension and may result in a costly repair. Don't leave the presser foot down when not in use on today's machines.

▶ "Universal" or "automatic" tension means that the machine uses a spring system that doesn't have to be adjusted every time you change threads and fabrics.

After leaving the tension assembly, the thread usually travels through one escapement before it enters the uptake. This is the part you see going up and down on every machine, the part that will hit you between the eyebrows if you lean forward far enough.

The Uptake

The uptake measures off portions of thread. If you watch the thread as you sew, you will see that the feed off the spool is not continuous and smooth, but piecemeal and somewhat random. The uptake's other job is to pull the thread up from the bobbin area. After leaving the uptake, the thread passes through other escapements, the number varying among machine brands. The one closest to the needle is important not to miss because it keeps the thread from fluttering, and causing skipped stitches.

Last but hardly least, the thread passes through the eye of the needle.

Lower Threading

The unseen parts below the throat plate complete the introduction to how a sewing machine makes a stitch.

The Shuttle, Race, and Hook

The "shuttle" defines the entire lower mechanism. The "race" is the part that moves around the bobbin casing. In a rotary machine it revolves in one circular direction; in an oscillator type, it rocks back and forth in semicircles. In either case, on the race is the "hook," which is a metal projection that picks up the incoming thread from the needle and spreads it over the bobbin casing to form the knot (Fig. 1.4).

Fig. 1.4

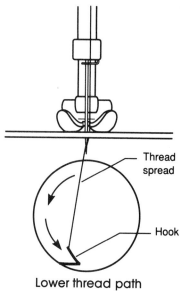

Thread spread

Hook

Lower thread path

Lower Tension Mechanism

The bottom tension is a spring-steel metal plate that presses against the casing that holds the bobbin in place. It is usually regulated by a tiny screw in the bobbin case or casing area. Its job is to anchor the lower thread in position so that the upper thread can make a stitch around it. That is also why the bottom mechanism is not as critical as the upper in terms of setting; it does very little in the process of stitch formation.

▶ Tightening the screw presses the plate more firmly against the casing, which makes the thread harder to pull out (Fig. 1.5). For firmer tension, tighten the screw (turn it to the *right*); for less pull, loosen it (to the *left*).

The direction that the bobbin thread winds into the casing area is not universal on all machines. Check your manual. Then make an arrow with an indelible marker to remind you of the proper direction.

▶ A bobbin case can wear out. If it just keeps getting looser, even though you've tightened it, use *Loctite* on the set screw, following manufacturer's instructions. Loctite is available in hardware stores. Better yet, buy a new bobbin case.

How a Machine Makes a Stitch

To learn how a machine functions and to lay the foundation for trouble-free sewing, I will first discuss the two troublesome *T*s—Timing and Tensions.

Fig. 1.5

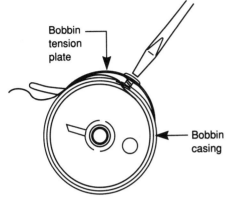

Bobbin tension plate

Bobbin casing

Bobbin tension plate presses against casing as screw is tightened

Fig. 1.6

Uptake at highest point

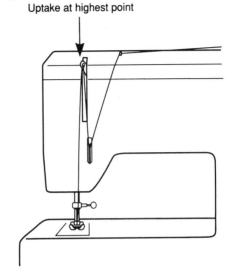

Beginning and end of a stitch

Timing

Timing is something that you truly cannot set up or repair yourself. I will explain what it is so that you can become a more informed consumer, but you really need an expert to do this repair.

Timing is critical, and bad habits can cause it to go out. Three functions must happen in sequence for a machine to make its stitch: the machine must move fabric, the needle must enter the fabric, and a knot must be formed. This is how it happens:

The feed dogs come up to move the fabric while the needle is out; in fact, the fabric can only move *while* the needle is out. The needle must not reenter the fabric until the feed dogs

have dropped. As the needle starts back up again and before it leaves the fabric, a loop of thread is formed. The hook then comes by, picks up this loop, and spreads it over the bobbin case or casing area. The hook's timing must be coordinated with the needle's upswing. The actual knot is made only when the needle is out of the fabric and the fabric is being moved forward by the feed dogs. **The ending and beginning of each stitch is when the uptake is at its highest point** (Fig. 1.6).

If any part of this sequence is out of order, a stitch cannot be formed. The main result of an improperly timed machine is a failure to produce stitches, period. The machine will not sew at all. (Other reasons for the machine's not forming a knot will be discussed later.)

If your machine goes out of time, please know that it is usually *your* fault, not the machine's. Only a poor-quality or damaged machine will go out of time.

Note: If you know that your sewing machine goes out of timing often, it may have been tooled from soft, poor-quality metal or plastic. If this happens, ask your repairmen to use Loctite on the set screws. It hardens up the area enough to hold a lock in place, but it loosens if cranked hard enough.

Tension

Perhaps the most common complaint heard in a repair shop is "the tension is off." More often than not, such a problem is caused by the machine's operator, not by the machine. What's more, it is a problem that you can solve yourself. Tensions rarely go out by themselves, no matter how inexpensive the machine. With the help of this book, you will learn that it is more likely an improper combination of needle, thread, and presser foot.

A definition of tension bears repeating and expanding. It is not complicated, although at first it may seem overwhelming. It is crucial to the understanding of stitch formation and how that relates to proper machine functioning:

Tension is the resistance against the thread throughout the machine. It is *not* only a function of the adjustments on the knob or dial at the front of the machine.

Without exception, two separating plates or disks comprise the upper tension assembly, even on the earliest machines. The lower tension mechanism is either a bobbin case (which may be located in various places) or a bobbin casing.

The needle comes down and enters the fabric. As it makes its next stitch, it is still attached to the previous one. The source of the thread for the next knot can either be from the spool by means of the uptake, or the needle can steal from the last stitch in the fabric. The machine's goal is to find the medium between the two, but it will *always* follow the line of least resistance if the two choices aren't equal. If the fabric is soft, for example, a machine at normal tension will pull from the last stitch, rather than from the spool, because it doesn't have to pull as hard or from as far away—in other words, the line of least resistance.

Fabric can act to stabilize the thread so that the machine can pull enough down from the spool to give the desired stitch length. But if the fabric is not firm enough, the thread will yank it back up. The softer the fabric, the more likely it will gather up. So you get puckers.

Adjusting the overall tension in the machine will result in knots forming evenly between the two layers of fabric on a straight stitch. What you want to achieve is equal tension, not equal pull.

The lower thread comes a short distance straight up from the bobbin, whereas the upper thread has a winding and longer route down from the spool. There is more drag on the upper thread because it must be pulled back up by the needle and the uptake, forming the knot.

Don't be concerned if this chapter is not clear yet. All this information is new to you and it will take some time to sink into your reality. Continue on and refer back to this chapter if necessary.

2

DON'T SPIT INTO YOUR SEWING MACHINE

Do you spit into your sewing machine to clean it out?

Although many of us will quickly answer "Not me!" most of us do blow into the machine to clear out the fuzz. Saliva contains enzymes that can actually erode the metal parts over time.

Instead, I find that a hair dryer works best. The warmth dissolves the oil already inside, making it easier to lift out, and there is enough air pressure to blow away looser bits hiding in the back.

> *Note:* The air propellant used in spray cans is cold, which coagulates the oil even more and only aggravates the problem. Also, the cold temperature can be so intense that it can actually damage parts.

The care of your machine, cleaning and oiling in particular, is the primary preventive measure you can take to ensure smooth machine function.

Although major repairs and problems still need the attention of a trained technician, there is much you can do at home. Most of it will not only save on repairs but will bring you closer to your machine and give you a greater feeling of control over "machine problems."

Cleaning Your Machine

For thorough internal cleaning, your best option is to use the brush that came with your machine. If you have lost it or never had one, buy or order another from your dealer. The best cleaning solvent is regular rubbing alcohol. Because it evaporates quickly, it doesn't promote rust. Dip your brush into it and remove the lint, old oil, and other buildup.

Rip an old soft cotton cloth into pieces and dip the torn edge of one piece into the alcohol. Run it gently between the separating disks of the upper tension mechanism (Fig. 2.1). Do this about every six months to remove any excess sizing, coating, dye, or other buildup that thread might have shed there. Be sure the presser-bar lifter is

Fig. 2.1

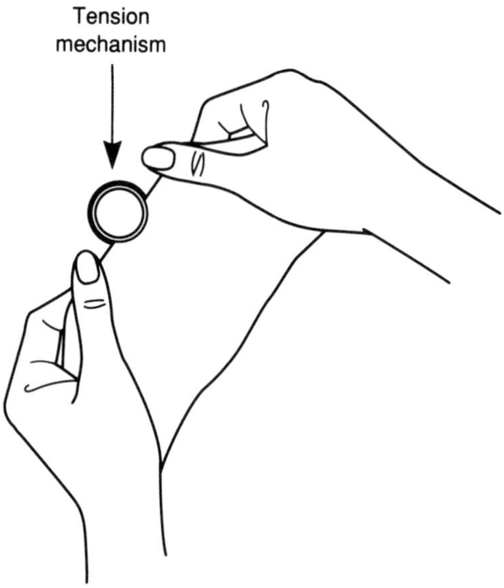

Tension mechanism

Clean separating disks with a soft cotton cloth dipped in rubbing alcohol

up so the disks are apart. If you have double disks (for two threads), be sure to clean on both sides. Try to clean as much of the metal portions of your machine as possible with this cloth.

Be sure to remove the throat plate, even if you must unscrew it. The fuzz that builds up there from shedding fabrics can actually act like a sponge, soaking up oil and becoming like concrete. When it is hard enough, it can actually stop the feed dogs from moving at all.

Note: Learn this important technique for removing these and other screws. When you put the screwdriver in the slot, put your other hand on top and press firmly while turning. This prevents marring the slot, stripping it, or making burrs (Fig. 2.2).

Fig. 2.2

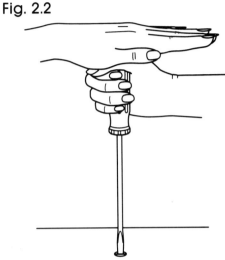

Use both hands to prevent marring the slot, stripping it, or making burrs

Never poke around the bobbin area or elsewhere with your seam ripper or other metal objects to "clean" it. You can create burrs or scratches, which will adversely affect the tension. *Remember:* When two pieces of metal come together, one of them is going to lose. The best items to use if you need to dig inside are bamboo skewers or orange sticks. Toothpicks are too weak.

Don't be afraid to unscrew the top and bottom of your machine to get inside for maintenance. *Caution:* In an oscillator machine, the bobbin case will lift out easily, so you can clean and oil inside the shuttle. A rotary casing does not come apart. Be sure you know which kind of machine you have before taking it apart. If your bobbin case is removable, take it out and clean it with rubbing alcohol.

The readily accessible areas should be cleaned before you start a project. The more difficult-to-reach areas should be cleaned about every six months, according to usage.

The outside of your machine should also be cleaned with rubbing alcohol. Normal household cleaners can leave a sticky residue if they seep inside. Dampen a soft cloth and wipe the surface.

Note: If you have an antique machine and wish to clean it, using alcohol on the black lacquer will remove the artwork. Instead, use Grumbacher's oil-paint cleaner, which you can find at any art supply or craft store.

Cleaning the Motor Brushes

If you think your machine has slowed down over the years and is running sluggishly, you may need to clean the carbon brushes in the motor, which may be dirty or seated improperly. To accomplish this, disengage the clutch inside the handwheel as if to wind a bobbin, depress the foot pedal for about 10 minutes, and run the motor until you hear a change in its whirr. (*Note:* If you have trouble loosening the clutch, see Gremmie No. 6 in Chapter 5.)

Remember: Always oil your machine after cleaning before you use it.

Oiling and Lubing

The most frequently asked question about care of the sewing machine is, "How often should I oil it?"

Depending on how often you sew and the fabrics you use, you will need to oil your machine approximately every six hours of running time: that is, the time you are actually sewing, not pinning or ironing.

Use only sewing machine oil in your machine. Do not use any all-purpose household oil such as 3-in-1. I once saw a machine that had been oiled with olive oil for ten years and finally had stopped working.

The best oil doesn't have to be the one that came with your machine, but it *must* be specifically for sewing purposes. The detergents in household oils leave tacky residues that one day will cause your machine to stop running. Even if you don't use your machine often, this kind of oil will coagulate.

Sewing machine oil, on the other hand, evaporates, even when the machine is idle. That's why you especially need to oil a machine that has not seen action for some time.

If the manufacturer of your machine doesn't recommend oiling, but it begins to make noise after a while, you can use a non-oil lubricant such as Tri-Flow. It is available in some sewing-machine stores, bicycle shops, and hardware stores.

Please refer to your manual to find the exact spots to oil. The part that needs to be oiled the most often, however, is the race. Because it takes two revolutions of the shuttle to make one stitch, the shuttle moves twice as fast as any other part. So this area needs to be oiled twice as often, or about every six to eight hours of running time. You will know when it needs to be oiled because it will sound clattery.

A good way to find out what places need to be oiled is to put the machine on its widest zigzag and longest stitch and hand-turn the wheel forward. Any part that moves needs to be oiled. Oil wherever two pieces of metal come together.

The machine should be oiled when the uptake is at its highest point. Machines are set up so that the internal workings line up for proper oiling at that point. Repeat this process about once a month.

Even though you don't need to use a lot of oil, it's a good idea to run a piece of scrap cloth through before starting your project to absorb any excess oil that might stain your good fabric.

Unless your manual specifies oiling the motor, never oil or drip oil into it. The sewing machine works via closed circuit. The power flows alternately to the top and bottom of the motor. If you oil it, you can complete the circuit and blow it up. Some older machines have special caps near the motor that lead directly to the bearing that needs oil, but they have nothing to do with oiling the motor itself. Your manual will specify what parts need to be oiled.

If your manual recommends lubing the gears, use the special sewing machine lube sold at most fabric stores. It is similar in consistency to Vaseline. Check your manual to see which areas to lube (Fig. 2.3). Lube them every six months to a year.

Do not use oil on the gears. Oiling can cause them to slip, and your machine will not work.

Fig. 2.3

Apply lubricant
between gears.

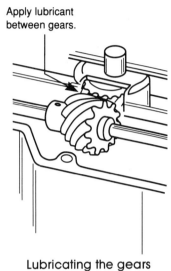

Lubricating the gears

You should have your machine professionally cleaned and lubed about every five to ten years whether you use it often or rarely. Over time, the solvents coagulate. A good repair shop will thoroughly strip your machine and clean places you are unable to reach.

Removing Burrs

A burr is a snag caused by a nick or hit from another piece of metal, such as a needle or seam ripper. It can cause jerky seams, snags in the fabric, or seams that don't feed straight or smoothly.

Now that you understand how important it is that the thread slide smoothly through the machine, you see how burrs can inhibit the progress of the thread as it travels through the machine and affect the quality of the stitches. That extra drag will affect the total gram weight of pull and throw off the tension.

It is important to check occasionally for burrs. Even tiny burrs can cause major problems with both sewing quality and sewing ease. You can find them in many places and for many reasons. The primary cause is the fabric puller—the sewer who reaches behind the bed of the machine and tugs on the fabric to "help" feed it through. If the fabric is pulled after the needle has entered it, the needle will bend back and strike the throat plate, often breaking. In the process, that action gradually chips away at the throat plate, causing burrs, especially at the back of the hole (Fig. 2.4).

Burrs can also be caused by broken needles that fall into the shuttle area. Check bobbins, bobbin cases, and presser feet for rough spots; they can occur here, too.

Burrs are best removed with a piece of crocus cloth, which is very fine sandpaper made of jeweler's rouge impregnated in fabric. It will smooth over the burrs without creating new rough spots. Beware of other sandpapers; none is as

Fig. 2.4

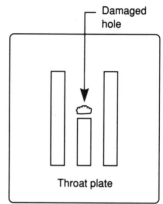

Fabric pull damage to throat plate

fine as crocus. You can buy crocus cloth at most hardware stores or lumberyards.

Run your fingers over all the metal parts of your machine. When you find a rough spot, remove it. Don't forget the shuttle area, even if burrs here are harder to find and remove. You may want to consider replacing the throat plate if it has too many burrs.

▶ Do not put a plastic cover over your machine to keep off the dust. Plastic actually makes the machine sweat, which encourages rusting of metal parts. Cover the machine with a towel or cloth instead. Never leave or store your needles and metal attachments in front of a window, where they might rust from frequent condensation.

Mechanical Repairs

After you've tried everything you know, including reading your manual and rethreading the machine, you may need to take it into the shop if it in fact isn't working. **Do not strip the machine before taking it in.** Don't remove the needle and don't remove the thread. Leave all the knobs in the positions they were in when the problem occurred. Do not remove the bobbin or its casing, and do not clean anything. Some people are embarrassed by taking in a dirty machine, but if you remove all the evidence, chances are the mechanic can't solve the mystery.

Take a scrap of the fabric you were working on when you had a problem to the shop. If the mechanic can get your machine to sew but you can't, you are probably doing something wrong. Feel free to ask about what repairs were made, but give the mechanic all the help you can by letting him see *how* you were sewing.

If you are in fact having operator problems, the rest of this book will help you improve your mind-set.

3

PEOPLE GET CHEAP IN THE STRANGEST PLACES

Do you change your sewing machine needle only when it breaks?

You put the time and the essence of yourself into your sewing, so why cheat yourself to save a few pennies?

The needle sews; the thread holds the garment or craft together. Yet these are the two places where people get incredibly cheap. The 30- or 40-cent-per-item investment is a small price to pay for the difference that quality notions make in the beauty of your project and the ease of your sewing. **Change your needle every two garments, or every twelve hours of actual sewing time.**

▶ You don't need to see the eye to thread the needle. If you follow the lengthwise groove down the front, it will guide your thread into the eye easily (Fig. 3.1).

Fig. 3.1

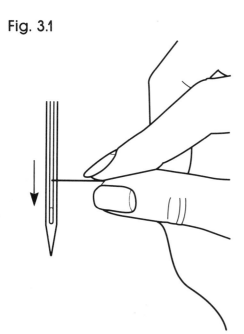

Slide thread down the groove to eye

The Evolution of Sewing Needles

Fabrics have changed more in the past twenty-five years than since we crawled out of skins and started wearing fabric clothes.

In the beginning, all we had were natural fibers and dyes—cotton, linen, wool, and silk. We had no need for specialized needles because these fabrics only had to touch the tip of the needle. All we needed were sharp points.

Twenty years ago, when we developed man-made fibers and dyes and polyester double-knits hit the market, the face of home sewing changed forever. But we had not learned to change our methods of sewing or to alter our home machines to work with these new fabrics. We weren't getting the same quality as we saw in commercial garments because the garment industry always adapts its machines to new fabrics well before the home market does. In fact, our home machines haven't changed much since 1895. They have been improved and have become infinitely more versatile, but they still form stitches in basically the same way.

The rash of polyester on the market created a mind-set of its own: Always use ballpoint needles with polyester to avoid skipped stitches.

But what is polyester? Is it wool-like, chiffon, a silkie? We need to stop thinking about fiber content and grab hold of what the manufacturers have done with it. In other words, don't look at the end of a bolt to read about fiber content as your only criterion for choosing which needles and threads to buy. You need to consider that, today, man-made fibers can be made to look like silk or wool. Crepe de chine, for example, can be silk, rayon, polyester, or even some other fiber. Concentrate on fiber usage, not content: Is it soft,

Fig. 3.2

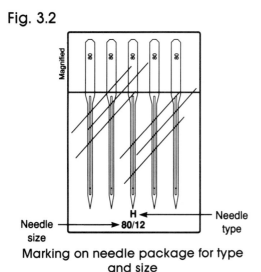

Marking on needle package for type and size

thick, dense, stiff? How will it handle? How does it feel?

This chapter will tell you what options are available and how to make sense of the problems that mismatches can cause. These considerations are why I am not giving any reference charts; there are no absolutes. Each project must be analyzed according to its own difficulties and requirements.

Every needle package will give you two classifications: the *number,* which denotes its thickness or size; and the *letter,* which specifies the point or tip and overall shape. It is the combination of size and shape that makes a needle best for any one piece of fabric.

I will use the Schmetz needle clas-sifications because, in my opinion, these are the best needles manufactured to-day. I will present all the numbers in pairs, starting with the most commonly used needle, the 80/12. The left num-ber is the European designation (milli-meters around); the figure on the right is the American standard (Fig. 3.2). I will discuss first the number, then the letter, of each series of Schmetz needle currently available. Check later in this chapter for special cases.

Selecting Needles by Number

You don't need to buy every kind of needle for every kind of fabric you might use. You will use the 60H, 70H, 80H, 75H-S and 90H-J most often. But when you do encounter problems, if you have a basic understanding of the structure of these other needles, you can increase your options for problem solving. See the closeup of machine needle in Fig. 3.3.

▶ 80/12

This needle is the most flexible for use in the middle range of fabric den-sities in both cotton wovens and knits. Today's standard is slightly smaller than

Fig. 3.3

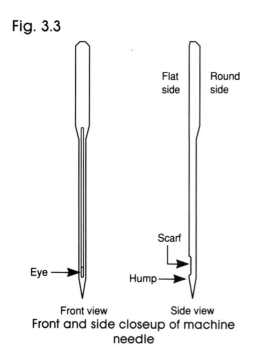

Flat side

Round side

Scarf

Eye →

Hump →

Front view   Side view

Front and side closeup of machine needle

that used in the "old" days. In the past we used big needles to prevent breakage, because they were comparatively expensive. But with the influx of many kinds of needles and more sophisticated fabrics, we have learned that we get the best quality stitch with the smallest possible needle for any given project.

▶ 90/14

This next larger needle is best used with denim, jeans, corduroy, most upholstery fabric, and canvas.

▶ 100/16

This needle is best for backed upholstery (such as Herculon) and very heavy or dense fabrics such as fake furs.

▶ 110/18, 120/20, and 130/22

Any time you use a needle larger than a 100/16, you are purposely creating a hole. These needles are fine for hemstitching, fagotting, and other decorative work. If you really want to create a hole, you can buy a wing needle, which is made only for this purpose.

> *Note:* Be aware of overkill. Do not automatically buy a larger needle, thinking that it will never break on thick fabrics. If the needle is thicker than the density of the fabric it must penetrate, it will break. Be aware also that using too big a needle on a piece of heavy fabric might force your machine out of timing.

▶ 70/10

This needle is best used for average light- to medium-weight fabrics such as voile, lighter dress fabrics, men's shirting, light cottons, and batiste.

▶ 65/9

These needles are relatively new. They are best used with crepe de chine weights, silkies (rayon, polyester), and real silk. This needle is the smallest you can use with standard-weight thread if you don't have finer thread.

▶ 60/8

This needle is best for very lightweight fabrics such as crepe de chine, charmeuse, satin, and chiffon. Don't forget that the eye of the needle is directly proportional to its circumference. Be sure to read the thread section to learn which weight is best used with this needle.

▶ 50/6

These needles are hard to find, but they sew wonderfully on real silk. Be aware that some of the cheap silk being sold today hasn't been adequately treated to remove the gummy residue that causes needles to stick while penetrating the fibers. These needles break easily, but they are the only ones that sew on *problematic*, extra-fine fabrics.

Selecting Needles by Letter

Thinking again about the evolution of fashion and the great changes in fabrics will help you understand the various letter classifications on needle packages (Fig. 3.4).

Fig. 3.4

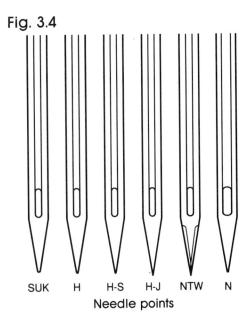

SUK   H   H-S   H-J   NTW   N

Needle points

When we had only natural fibers, we bought needles by size alone. They all had sharp points. Then we had polyester double-knits and used only ballpoints. Today we have as many kinds of needles as varieties of fabric. This change is also why you can't buy needles according to what you were taught twenty years ago. Now we must also consider the needle's overall shape.

I will start with the letter "H" or "universal," meaning that it works on the broadest group of fabrics.

▶ H

The Schmetz H series denotes a point or shape that is neither strictly sharp nor ballpoint. It is an all-purpose needle point for most knits and wovens. It is barely rounded at the tip and has a scarf. The point is universal to most fabrics.

Since there are exceptions, your best rule of thumb is: If in doubt, make a test seam with the same fabric, needle, and thread you will use in your project. You can start with the 80/12 H as a base, since this is the needle you will use most of the time.

▶ H-S

The sharp points worked fine until the advent of polyester knits. When stretch and density were added, the industry had to change the shape of the needle as well as its thickness.

The problem for home sewers in using the sharp points with knits and stretchier fabrics was skipped stitches. The fibers would catch on the end of the needle and be carried down into the bobbin area so that no loop of thread could be formed to make the stitch.

The industry solved the problem at first by inventing the ballpoint needle. The first big lie "they" told you was that all polyester fabric needed ballpoint needles. The tip was redesigned with a rounded point, so the thread would slide off the tip, allowing a stitch to be made. The bad news, however, was that the ballpoint needle produced holes along the seams of the garment after it had

been washed. These holes were particularly visible on Qiana-like fabrics.

A new needle for knits was necessary. So manufacturers left the H point to prevent the holes, and redesigned the scarf and hump so the needle would have a better chance of making a stitch. The H-S series works well on most knits without damaging the seam line.

The "S" denotes "stretch," and the needles come in 75/11 and 90/14 sizes. The smaller is best for lingerie and other stretchables that need to be pulled onto the body, such as T-shirt knits. The larger is best for double-knits.

Remember: Ultrasuede is a knit and takes a 75 H-S needle. If you use a 90 H-S, you will create a hole to last forever.

▶ SUK

There are still a few times that the ballpoint needle, denoted by the letters "SUK," will be necessary. Fabrics with spandex, some elastic waistbands and other elastics, and occasional knits that won't respond to any other needle are the best examples.

▶ H-J

A few years ago we started seeing the return to natural fibers and the popularity of jeans. So the industry had to reinvent the wheel: they had to bring back sharp needles to penetrate the tightly woven, dense fibers. So they began making the H-J (J for jeans) series. They painted them blue and now they cost more, but the scarf is basically the same as the H series, although the point is sharp. They come in 90s, 100s, and 110s, larger-than-standard sizes, and are used for extraordinarily dense fabrics such as upholstery and canvas. In fact, whenever you want a 90 or 100 needle, you should automatically buy an H-J.

▶ **N series**

Have you ever done topstitching and gotten wads or loops underneath? The reason is, if the thread is thicker than the eye of the needle it can't slide properly and be pulled back up as the stitch is formed. The N series is made specifically for topstitching. It comes in 80s and 90s, and has a double-size eye. It is best used with topstitching thread, although you may double-thread it with standard-weight thread for similar results.

▶ **NTW series**

Real leather or suede takes the NTW needle, which comes in 80s, 90s, 100s, and 110s. They have a wedge point, which slits the hide instead of making a hole. If you use a normal needle, the fabric will heal itself around the hole before the needle pulls back, making skips and loops underneath. Do not use on synthetic suede or leather.

▶ **Double needles**

Double or twin needles are meant for decorative work, primarily on fine fabrics. They are not meant for top-stitching on woven fabric because the back is a zigzag. Don't forget that top-stitching on commercially made jeans is done by a special machine with two separately functioning needles, not a double needle.

Double needles do excellent top-stitches on knits. The zigzag back gives stretch; the front looks like straight stitching. Double needles do not come in ballpoint, which will cause skipped stitches on some fabrics.

> *Hint:* When using double needles, if you want the seams to lay flat, you must loosen your bottom tension mechanism almost all the way. Otherwise, you will get minitucks. However, if you want those tucks to show up even more, tighten the lower mechanism.

Special Cases

Singer or Yellow/Gold Band

If you have a Singer that skips a lot on many different fabrics—and *only* then—you need the Gold or Yellow

Band series. The company adapted this needle so that it moves closer to the hook while forming the stitch, reducing the chance for skips. Many Singers will work well with the Schmetz needles, but Gold or Yellow Band needles are not recommended for use in European machines.

Bernina B

The manufacturer recommends using the B needles for Berninas prior to the 900 series. If you have found that your machine skips stitches with other needles, you may need to use the B series. They have less scarf and work better with the Bernina hook design. They come in normal, sharp, and ballpoints and are available only through Bernina dealerships.

To determine whether your machine takes B or H needles, you must experiment. You can almost always use the B; however, if your machine will function with the H series, you will find a broader range to choose from and greater availability.

Viking and Elna

There is no such animal as a Viking or Elna needle per se. They are all made by Schmetz, who then sometimes puts another name across the package. Most European machines use

Schmetz needles, which are also manufactured in Europe.

▶ Specialized needles are more likely to be found in sewing machine stores than in fabric stores. This is also true for attachments and better-quality threads.

The Evolution of Thread

There is no economy in buying cheap thread. Why buy the 5/$1 thread in a bin if it ends up costing you a $25 trip for a repair? Bad thread may have been the sole source of your problem.

Needles and thread are the two most important variables in your sewing because they come in direct contact with your fabric. I cannot overstate this fact. You spend so much time creating something beautiful, why ruin it with cheap thread? You need to start looking at and feeling the thread you buy. Is it smooth, so that it will slide easily through the eye of the needle? Or is it rough and full of slubs that will catch and cause it to break?

In the beginning, when all we had were natural fibers, the only thread needed was 100 percent cotton. It sewed beautiful seams, and we didn't much think about it. Then when polyester double-knits became popular, sewers who used the cotton thread with it experienced much breakage.

Polyester knit was and is a stretch fabric, the first of its kind on the market. So polyester thread was invented, which at the time was the easiest way to cure the breakage problems. This thread had a certain amount of stretch and wouldn't pucker on stiff, nongiving fabrics.

Then we slipped into the polyester mind-set: The second big lie was to always use polyester thread with polyester fabric. And until recently there was so much polyester thread on the market that cotton had all but disappeared. We had little choice of which thread to use.

The truth is, sewing machines were invented to be used with cotton thread (and they still do function best with it). Even so, our fabrics and tastes keep changing. We were introduced to T-shirts and other single knits and began to see puckers along the side seams. We got around the problem by stretching the material as we sewed, which actually stretched out the formation of the stitches so that the thread had some give when we let go.

Now we are returning to natural fibers—soft fabrics that give, move, and work up differently than man-made fibers. If we still use polyester thread with them, we will get puckers. Most polyester thread has a lot of stretch to it. Because tension is resistance against the thread, it stretches out polyester thread like a rubber band as it moves through the machine. Then when the thread is sewn into the garment, it relaxes back into its original state, puckering the fabric with it.

Manufacturers can make acrylic look like wool, linen look like cotton, and polyester look like silk. So it isn't a matter of whether to use polyester or cotton thread as such; what is relevant is whether the fabric is thin, stiff, resistant, soft—in other words, how it handles. In all cases you want the thickness of the thread to approximate the thickness of the garment fibers as closely as possible.

Cotton Thread

Cotton thread is more flexible than polyester thread, so it's wonderful for buttonholes and satin stitching because it doesn't stretch. Thus it won't pucker as much as polyester on the zigzag stitch.

Cotton thread makes the smoothest, best seams. Cotton is absolutely the best for dressmaking. Its tendency to dry out has given it a bad reputation, but it can be rehydrated in the crisper section of your refrigerator. Don't put it in the frost-free compartment, as that encourages dryness. (That's why museums use humidifiers; many tapestries and documents, including the Declaration of Independence, have been preserved this way.)

Before discussing specific sizes and weights of thread, it is important to mention that measurements have never been standardized. What one company calls "double zero" another calls "50 weight" and yet another calls "30 weight." Most companies give no ratings.

For a frame of reference, I will use Mettler thread, because it features an understandable grading system. It is also among the best on the market today, and it's widely distributed.

Mettler makes several varieties of cotton thread for general sewing and two types of standard weight. One is referred to as machine-embroidery weight, noted as 30/2 (30 weight/2 ply). It comes in a wide range of colors and is Mettler's softest cotton thread; 30/2 has a tendency to be fuzzy and is best used for crafts, such as appliqué and machine embroidery.

The other is called "silk finish" or (50 weight/3 ply). The name refers to the high-luster sheen, not the fiber content, as it is made of 100% cotton. It is used for everyday sewing. In most cases you will want to use it for the smoothest seams on most normal-weight fabrics.

If your thread is chubbier than your fabric, you will have lumpy seams. The knots will always show more on thin fabrics. To solve this predicament, Mettler also makes a "fine machine embroidery" weight thread, designated 60/2. It is best for those fine fabrics that may have always given you trouble. It is half the weight of normal thread and therefore flows right into the fabric, hiding the seams. For example, this thread works beautifully on silk and silkies, specifically at a stitch length of "2" or "14" (stitches per inch).

I do not recommend using the fine-weight thread with anything but a size 60 or 50 needle. If you use it in a larger size, it will not fill the eye properly. If it isn't held tight against the groove, the needle will break when punched down into the fabric.

When you use the 50s and 60s needles, you *must* use fine-weight machine-embroidery thread. If the thread thickness is larger than the eye of the needle, it will produce poor-quality seams because it can't slide through smoothly. It is also very hard to thread.

There are several other good brands of cotton thread: Swiss Zwicky, and Coats and Clark ONT are two. Check what is available to you locally, as well as the Supply List at the end of the book. (These better threads are often used in machine demonstrations because they produce such beautiful stitches.)

Polyester Thread

Polyester thread has three basic uses: (1) in garments that will receive stress, such as leotards or the rear end of pants; (2) on fabrics that will be exposed to elements, such as swimwear and furniture; and (3) on real leather, because the tannic acid will eat away at cotton thread that hasn't been specially treated.

The primary reason for using polyester rather than cotton thread is its strength. Although its stretchiness can be a disadvantage, in these cases it is better than cotton because it won't break. The strength of the seam is more important here than how it looks.

The way that polyester thread is made determines its quality. Many companies make it by a process similar to that of cotton candy. It is pulled on and run through a series of heat rings until the outside shrinks down. If you could look through a microscope, however, you would see slubs and fuzz rather than smooth strands. In cheap thread, these chunks catch on the eye of the needle. These imperfections can cause more frustrations than you may realize.

The best polyester threads are made of continuous filaments and then twisted. Metrosene and Gütermann, both made in Europe, are two of the finest.

Metrosene, for example, is 100 percent long staple polyester. It is made on cones that pull out the strands over a long space. This makes for a smooth thread that travels easily through the machine.

Cotton-wrapped polyester thread is the worst of both worlds. Several kinds are available today, but some are better than others. To find out which is best, take a bit of thread off the spool and look at it. Check it for slubs; pull on it to see how rubbery it is. The more give, the more problems it will cause. You don't want to use thread that stretches out as you sew, only to snap back to original size once in the garment. The seams will look terrible.

Sometimes you won't be able to find the exact color you need in either cotton or polyester thread. If you must choose between good quality or exact color match, **choose good thread.** A lousy seam will look bad whether the color matches or not; a good seam will hide an imperfect color match. Manufacturers buy in such large quantities that their threads are dyed to match. That option is not open to home sewers. Don't hold an entire spool against your fabric. Instead, unwind a few inches and use a single strand to check the match. Try dark gray for those difficult purples and blues.

> *Note:* Do not use polyester thread on silk. (It is four to seven times stronger than silk.) If you do, you will wear a garment that looks as if it were sewn with bandsaws. In fact, when working on thin fabrics, remember that you are hardly going to play basketball in them. The seams don't have to be as strong as those in jeans.

Silk Thread

Silk thread was created for hand sewing. It is not recommended for home machine use. It is wonderful for hand-sewn hems and pad stitching because it is so strong and can't be easily broken. (It can shred but rarely breaks.) It has much greater tensile strength than cotton thread, and it doesn't knot because it is made from one extremely long, continuous filament.

This brings up another mind-set that misleads consumers: **Silk thread is not to be sewn into silk fabrics.** It is too strong, even for most wovens. It

could be used, for instance, in a particularly heavy wool coat that had to be dry cleaned and needed a strong seam. But that is a rare exception.

Topstitching Thread or Buttonhole Twist

Topstitching threads are available in both silk and polyester. For best results, you must use a topstitching needle. If you use this thread and have trouble with it jamming underneath, it is because it's too thick to be pulled back up with normal tension. Tighten the upper mechanism to add enough resistance to allow the thread to be brought back up to form a stitch instead of wadding below.

> *Note:* Don't put topstitching thread in the bobbin. Its thickness can ruin the tension mechanism. Use normal-weight thread instead. Consider using two standard-weight threads instead of one thick one in both the needle and bobbin areas. In the upper tension mechanism there is usually a separation disk; guide one thread to each side. For the bottom, wind two threads at a time onto your bobbin.

Thread Notes

The machine is carefully set up to balance upper and lower tensions, so you must put the same thread in both mechanisms (except for topstitching thread). Take the thread from the same spool. If you can't tell the difference between polyester and cotton by feel, devise a system to keep them apart during storage. Even if two threads seem to look alike, if one is smoother, it could mean enough of a difference in gram weight of pull to throw off the tension.

Commercial-weight thread, especially thread recommended for upholstery, is not made to go through a normal home sewing machine. If you use too thick a thread, you can actually damage both tension assemblies. Look for threads in home sewing stores that state "For Hand Sewing Only." Check the ends of your spools.

Don't take for granted that the thread you bought yesterday is still made with the same standards today. Be aware of the quality of thread you buy. There are unmentionable examples in which a brand started out with high quality but once the name was established, the standards dropped dramatically.

If you're sewing with a dark brown thread, for example, and suddenly have trouble, try switching brands to see if that helps if nothing else seems to work. This problem stems from poor-quality dyes. A variety of problems can occur when thread standards drop. Test by inserting a thread that you have used successfully before.

In fact, until you as a consumer find out what thread you ought to be using and ask for it, stores will continue to sell junk. Experiment until you are satisfied. Poor-quality thread is causing more puckers today than ever.

4

FOOT NOTES AND FEED DOGS

No matter what fabric you're using or what technique, do you always sew with the presser foot that came on the machine when you bought it? Feet make a tremendous difference in the ability of your machine to make good quality stitches and especially to keep a balanced tension. Using the wrong foot for a certain fabric, for example, can actually throw off the tension and cause problems that you might be tempted to blame on "the tension" or on a crummy sewing machine.

The presser foot either holds the fabric against the feed dogs firmly or it doesn't. If the fabric isn't firmly held, you will get flutter. If the fabric can shift easily, it won't offer the necessary resistance against the thread to form stitches with correct tension.

All-Purpose Feet

Fig. 4.1

Regular or standard foot

Satin stitch or embroidery foot
Comparing standard and satin stitch feet

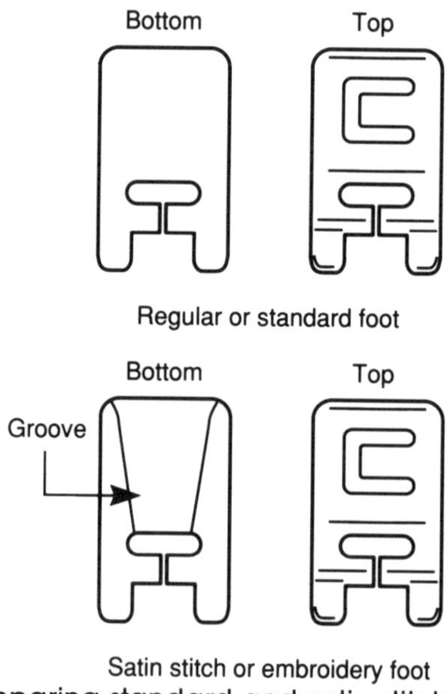

Only two types of presser feet can be called "all-purpose": (1) the standard sewing foot and (2) the satin-stitch or embroidery foot (Fig. 4.1). Both are used in all phases of sewing to create different effects on the fabric. Don't confuse these feet with specialty or one-purpose feet, such as a buttonhole foot.

When you pick up a presser foot, take a look at the bottom as well as the top. It is the *bottom* that comes in contact with the fabric while the feed dogs are moving it.

The standard foot is flat all across the opening toward the back so that the fabric can ease up under it. It is almost always metal, and its purpose is to hold the material firmly and evenly all the way across the feed dogs. This is the foot that came on the machine, and although you will use it much of the time, it does have limitations.

That's why the satin-stitch foot was created. If you turn it over to look at the bottom, you will notice a groove down the center from front to back. This indentation allows the foot to slide over the buildup of thread from satin stitching, without getting caught up and creating mountains. The satin-stitch foot is usually plastic.

If you were to use the all-purpose foot for satin stitching, there would be no room for the buildup of stitches to pass through smoothly.

Sometimes, however, you may want to use these presser feet for something other than their appointed purposes. These other uses create the appearance of different kinds of tension.

For example, if you are sewing on squooshy fabric such as soft sweatshirting and you don't want those ruffled seams, you can use the satin-stitch foot. The groove allows the fabric enough room to pass through without being pressed so tight that it squeezes out around the feed dogs, only to recoil again when released. This foot allows the fabric to keep its shape while being sewn, with enough pressure not to cause skipped stitches from flutter.

On some machines you can loosen the pressure regulator to accomplish this purpose, but if possible, change to the embroidery foot instead. The more firmly the fabric is held against the outside edges of the foot, the more smoothly the feed dogs will move. The two methods don't exactly perform the same operation, but the results are similar.

Perhaps you're thinking, "OK, I don't ever want ruffly seams, so I'm only going to use the satin-stitch foot."

Wrong.

If you remember how stitches are made, you know that as the needle pulls out of a piece of fabric the stitch is formed. If you use the satin-stitch foot all the time, especially on lighter fabrics that can flutter, then when that fabric moves up with the needle into the groove of the foot, the little thread bubble won't form underneath. Instead, you will get skipped stitches (Fig. 4.2). The movement in that free space in the foot will also encourage puckers.

▶ If you are in fact experiencing skips and puckers and don't know why, check your presser feet. They are *not* interchangeable; they have different purposes. Make sure you are using the right one.

Fig. 4.2

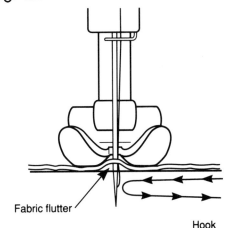

How stitches skip when wrong foot is used

Specialized Feet

Many alternate feet are available to expand the range and enjoyability of sewing projects. A few, however, need special mention. They are single-purpose feet and are not interchangeable.

Buttonhole Foot

Whether you have a simple zigzag machine or a new automatic one, if you want to make a buttonhole, you must use a buttonhole foot (Fig. 4.3).

Buttonholes are two parallel lines of satin stitching that must be lined up carefully and have enough space between to be cut open. When you use an

Fig. 4.3

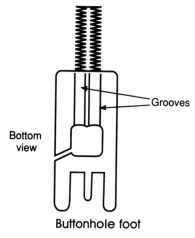

Bottom
view

Buttonhole foot

Fig. 4.4

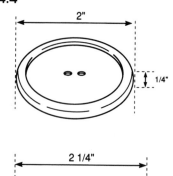

2"

1/4"

2 1/4"

Buttonhole opening measures one width,
plus one thickness

all-purpose foot, the bulk of threads from a row of stitching forms enough resistance to keep the machine from moving the fabric forward at all, or at least to make it slide off to one side. A buttonhole foot has special grooves on the bottom or an open space to allow the first row a place to rest while the second row is being formed.

Some new buttonhole feet will fit on your machine to measure the buttonhole for you. You need to ask around. If your machine has a built-in buttonhole—that is, it will stitch down one side and automatically reverse at the adjustment of a mechanical knob—you can now buy a foot that will actually measure the button and show you where to stop, instead of just sliding along with the fabric (Fig. 4.4).

These new feet also make corded buttonholes. You would use them to reinforce jeans buttonholes or on sweater knits or stretch fabrics to keep the buttonholes from stretching out of shape. Each foot works basically the same way, but there are variations. Ask the salesperson from whom you buy it.

I recommend looking at the newest feet. They are longer, have some space to see the opening, and have some kind of measuring device (Fig. 4.5). Because they are long, however, and because you usually sew along the edge of the garment, the fabric won't move forward because the weight falls to the

Fig. 4.5

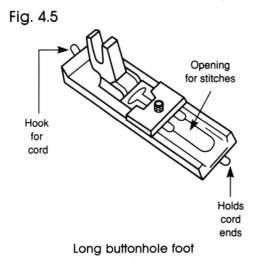

Opening for stitches

Hook for cord

Holds cord ends

Long buttonhole foot

back of the foot. With these longer feet (if they stick out more than an inch in front), it is a good habit to put your finger on the front end to keep it from bouncing. Don't push or shove; simply make a counterweight so the entire foot presses firmly onto the feed dogs.

You must use interfacing for a professional-looking buttonhole. If the pattern or fabric demands a buttonhole in an area where interfacing would be inappropriate, you may use a removable stabilizer. The newest on the market are plastic-like, water-soluble products used primarily for appliqué. If your fabric is white, you might try a paper backing. Some patterns use a third layer of fabric.

Don't forget that a buttonhole is a zigzag, so it *can* produce tunneling. You may need to decrease your upper and lower tensions to avoid puckering on finer fabrics. Also, be careful to pinch the threads when you pull out your finished work or you will wind up with one side puckered.

Beware of the super-automated buttonhole feature on the new computer machines. It doesn't allow for variable thicknesses and placements of buttonholes. If you can't override the programming, you won't have the flexibility needed when you encounter a problem.

Be realistic about what your buttonholes will look like made with a home machine. The two sides will never look identical because one side is coming forward and the other is going back up; they are not mirror opposites. You want to make the sides as evenly spaced as possible between stitches, but don't expect them to look the same. The machine cannot do it.

You may have been taught years ago to go around the buttonhole twice for that "perfect satin stitch" look. This mind-set prevents you from seeing that such a heavy buttonhole neither buttons well nor looks professional.

Remember: Your goal is to create a good-looking overall garment, not perfect individual sections. If you were as picky about the clothes you buy as the ones you make, you'd be naked most of the time.

Fig. 4.6

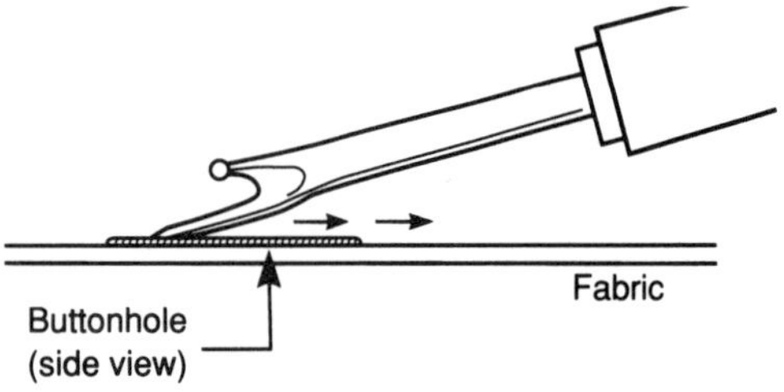

Buttonhole
(side view)

Fabric

Scrape edge of seam ripper down center
of closed buttonhole to separate threads

Fig. 4.7

Pin prevents accidentally cutting through
bar tacks

Here are several suggestions for opening the finished buttonhole. First, what is commonly called a seam ripper is in reality the buttonhole knife. By scraping its nonsharp edge three or four times down the center of the closed buttonhole to separate the threads, it will open easily and you won't cut the sides (Fig. 4.6). If you have a tendency to be strong-armed, put a pin across the bar tacks so that you can't cut through them (Fig. 4.7).

Fig. 4.8

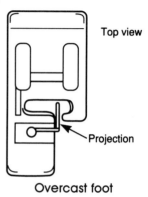

Top view

Projection

Overcast foot

For heavier fabrics such as leather or several layers of wool and interfacing, investigate a buttonhole chisel.

Overcast Foot

If you have a simple zigzag machine with no possibility of making the serpentine stitch and you want to do a full-width zigzag at the edge of a fabric, consider buying an overcast foot. This foot has a projection that stabilizes the thread until the machine makes its stitch, which prevents tunneling even on very light fabrics (Fig. 4.8).

Blind-Hem Foot

You can obtain a blind-hem stitch by machine that's as invisible as by hand, but there is a trick. The reason the dimple shows so much by machine is not because the bite is deeper, but because

Fig. 4.9

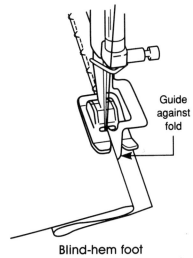

Guide against fold

Blind-hem foot

Fig. 4.10

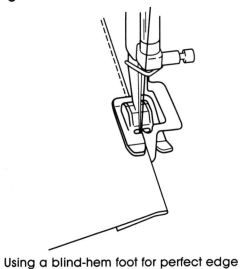

Using a blind-hem foot for perfect edge stitching

the amount of pull necessary for a normal seam is too firm for a blind hem. If you loosen the upper tension mechanism so that the knot falls to the back and the thread doesn't pull against the hem, making that dimple, you will have a professional-looking stitch using the blind-hem foot (Fig. 4.9). *Remember:* The goal is to arrive at a beautiful hem as seen from the *outside,* not perfect stitches on the inside.

The guide on this foot also helps make the seam straight. This means it's useful for straight edgestitching. Just place the guide at the edge of the seam and you will have even lines and speedy sewing (Fig. 4.10).

Zipper Foot

Zipper feet are made to hold one side of any project that has a lump— for example, the teeth of a zipper or cording. The foot is designed to sew completely clear of that lump. But many of the newer feet, especially snap-on ones, hang up on the very areas they should be avoiding.

Please check that your zipper foot either works correctly or that your shank is of universal standard so that you may purchase a foot that does work. The shank portion of most snap-off feet is itself removable, so other standard feet can be used.

Shanks

Fig. 4.11

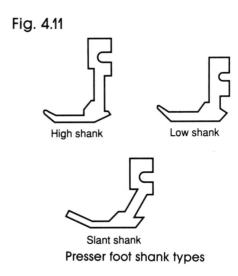

High shank   Low shank

Slant shank
Presser foot shank types

Speaking of feet, we must also talk about shanks. A shank is the part of the foot that attaches to the machine.

Shanks are made in three standard heights; high shank, which measures about 1″ from the base of the foot to the screw-on portion; low shank, about 1/2″ and is the "most standard"; and slant shank, which is for slant-needle machines (Fig. 4.11).

Too many changes have occurred over the years, even within the same company, to give a chart of absolutes as to which companies make which shanks. For example, Kenmore makes every kind of shank, depending on the year and manufacturer. You must know your machine's model and number when you buy feet and optional attachments. Your best bet is to take your manual and standard sewing foot with you.

Today more machines use the snap-off rather than the screw-on feature for attaching presser feet. In this case you must also unscrew the shank portion and take it and the standard foot with you to be sure you buy the correct-size attachments.

I caution you to make sure any machine you purchase can be fitted with one of the three common shank types. Several machines on the market today have nonstandard shanks that limit attachments to those that come with the machine. If a new, helpful, or interesting foot is developed, or if you need a special one, you will not be able to use it on your machine.

Bernina, by the way, is an animal unto itself, with its own shank design. But the company also makes an adaptor that attaches to other standard, low-shank feet.

Feed Dogs

Since feed dogs are the real movers and shakers of the sewing machine, you need to know how to use them to your advantage. You must next understand how feed dogs relate to presser feet and to the total tension in your machine on any given project.

Feed dogs are those tooth-like or pyramid-like projections that grab the fabric from under the foot and move it forward or backward. For the best seams and decorative work, you want as much fabric as possible in contact with the feed dogs.

For the fabric to move at all, the needle must come down and enter the fabric just as the feed dogs drop or stop moving. In other words, the needle must enter when the fabric is stationary.

Most of us don't take into account the motion and function of the feed dogs when we sew. We assume that the layers automatically move through together. But we know that in the race between the layers, the bottom one usually wins. We've gotten to the end of the seam, and the top layer is 1/2″ to 1″ longer. This is because the feed dogs push up against the lower layers and grip it more firmly than the top layer.

The way you hold the fabric can aggravate the uneven feed. Placing your fingers on the top of the fabric creates more drag on that layer, allowing the bottom layer to move through even faster. You can control the feed by putting one hand under the fabric, barely holding it in place with your thumb on top, and lifting it slightly just in front of the foot. That puts more drag on

Fig. 4.12

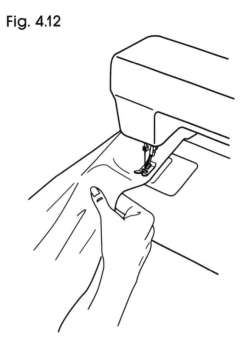

Control feed by lifting fabric slightly

the bottom layer and assures a more even feed.

There are times when you can use this idiosyncracy to your advantage, however. When sewing a piece where the pattern suggests easing in one layer, for instance, or when you know one layer is longer, then put that layer on the bottom and let the natural action of the feed dogs take over. The longer layer will be pulled through first with each stitch movement. The two will come out even, without puckers or pleats. You can, with practice, go so far as to hold onto the top layer and almost gather in the bottom to obtain an even feed.

> *Note:* When the feed dogs move the fabric, you can't expect them to push more than two layers through at one time and maintain quality. I suggest "two-by-two" sewing, meaning that you sew only two layers at a time. If you must put four layers together, such as in a collar, sew two together first, then the other two. Then treat them as one each and sew them together.

Feed dogs can wear out, especially the rubber ones made in the late 1960s when knits were popular. The rubber allowed the fabric to move through without damage. Once the rubber hardens and becomes slick as it dries out, it can't move any material. You can replace rubber feed dogs fairly inexpensively.

Metal feed dogs rarely wear out unless the metal was of poor quality. If so, they can flatten out over time and will no longer grab the fabric. The pyramid-shaped feed dogs, by the way, hold the fabric much tighter than the tooth-like projections. These metal feed dogs can also be replaced, unless they were welded onto the machine.

When doing free-hand machine embroidery or monogramming, you may want to dispense with the feed dogs entirely. In some machines they can be lowered mechanically; in others a cover plate is required. You can also set the stitch length at zero and ignore the feed dogs.

Bobbins

The importance of a carefully wound bobbin cannot be overemphasized. If the thread is not smooth and even on the bobbin, your stitches will not form properly.

To wind the bobbin properly, first take a look at the bobbin itself. The bobbin should have a hole through which you can run the thread up from the inside out. Hold onto the thread firmly, depress the pedal slowly and the threads will twist off, leaving no excess thread on the outside of the bobbin, which also can throw off the tension (Fig. 4.13).

Always rest a finger on the top of the spool of thread to ensure a smoothly wound bobbin. You may have to help guide the thread with your finger for an even wind; no machine is made with an absolutely perfect bobbin winder. (In fact, that's one of the things we gave up in the evolution of sewing. Today's machines are more versatile, but they don't wind the bobbins nearly as well.)

Fig. 4.13

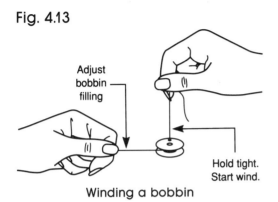

Adjust bobbin filling

Hold tight. Start wind.

Winding a bobbin

Note: There is no such thing as a universal bobbin. If it doesn't fit your machine, don't buy it. Bobbins are milled to fit exactly so that the tension will be in balance; improperly fitting bobbins will throw off the tension. Although many brands seem similar in size, make sure you know which size yours requires.

Any method of filling the bobbin through the eye of the needle will have inherent disadvantages caused by the characteristics of thread. All thread contains slubs, and when they catch on the eye in this method of winding, you risk an improperly wound bobbin.

Can you bring thread directly from the needle across to the top (for a top- or side-winding bobbin) to eliminate having to unthread the machine? Yes, you can do it. No, it is never a good idea because of slubs in the thread.

If your bobbin winds with difficulty, your rubber bobbin-winder tire may be worn out. The tire can be easily replaced.

Be on the alert: Even the smallest crack or burr on a bobbin can wreak havoc with your stitches. Be especially suspicious of the plastic variety; often the problem is not easily seen. If in doubt, throw it out, or at the very least, try a new one.

Knob Knotes

Stitch Length

Stitch length is the dial on your machine that measures the distance between stitches. It is expressed in one of two ways: millimeters between stitches (mm), generally 0 to 4; or stitches per inch, from 6 to "fine."

A basic stitch length for general sewing is about 2 1/2 mm or 12 to 15 stitches/inch. The measurements are not consistent with all fabrics; it is an average measured for a hard-finish, medium-weight fabric.

Thick fabric needs a longer stitch length than thinner material does to achieve the same distance between the knots. Wool and fleece need a longer stitch to cover the same territory because they have so much more resist-

Fig. 4.14

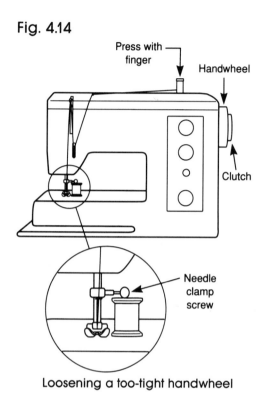

Loosening a too-tight handwheel

Note: If you sometimes don't have the strength to release the clutch on the handwheel in order to wind a bobbin, try this method: Take an old (wooden) spool of thread and place it under the needle-clamp screw (with the foot unattached), with the presser-bar lifter down. When you bring the handwheel forward, this maneuver should give you enough leverage to release the clutch (Fig. 4.14). It also helps to use a rubber jar lid to get a grip on the wheel knob. Remember, right is tight, so turn the knob to the left, or toward you.

Fig. 4.15

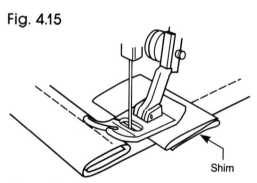

Use a shim to create even sewing height over thick seams

ance to being moved. In other words, thick fabrics don't move as easily between the feed dogs and the presser foot. Fine fabrics actually sneak through the feed area more quickly; that's why they sew best seams at a length of 2 mm or 15 to 18 stitches per inch.

Remember that the thread for each stitch is either yanked off the spool by the uptake, or it tries to pull back some of the thread from the previous stitch. That's why the stitch length needs to be adjusted according to the texture of the fabric. A general rule of thumb is, the thinner the fabric, the shorter the stitch length. As thin fabric is moved forward, it doesn't have the strength or resistance to hold onto the thread until the machine makes its next stitch. So, unless the stitches are short, it puckers.

Conversely, a stiff fabric will help stabilize the previous stitch before the machine makes the next one, so you can use a longer stitch length and not get puckers.

A machine is set up to pull down 4 mm of thread for its longest possible stitch length. As that is its maximum, there's no more give at that point. Longer stitches therefore have no slack with which to withstand a jerk, so they can break apart more easily. As stitches get shorter, there is more slack between the knots because they're not at maximum tautness. So if you want fewer puckers and more give, shorten your stitch length.

> *Note:* When using longer stitch lengths, loosen the upper tension mechanism so the knots fall to the bottom. Then the fabric won't pull up and pucker.

Needle Position

Needle position is greatly underestimated for its ability to obtain the best possible stitches. It has many uses but is not a feature on every machine.

For example, accurate, straight stitching lines are always a challenge for edgestitching and 1/4″ seams. Peo-

Fig. 4.16

Right needle position

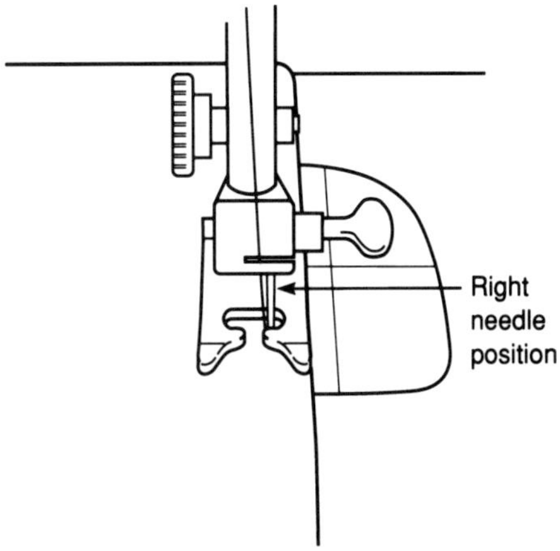

Move the needle, rather than fabric

ple usually move the fabric to the left to achieve this end. If instead you can move the needle to the left or right as needed (Fig. 4.16) and use the outer right edge of the foot as the guide, the feed will be more even and the lines will be straight. The sewing will also proceed more quickly.

It is difficult to find a guide for accurate edgestitching, and it is especially hard for the machine to push through evenly if the feed dogs are in contact with only a portion of the fabric. The foot has a tendency to fall off the edge, looking for less resistance, so you end up with wavy stitch lines. Again, if you have this option on your machine, move the needle instead of the fabric.

Remember: For the most professional work, as much fabric as possible must come into contact with the feed dogs.

Needle position is also useful for machines without a single-hole needle plate. When you want to work on finer fabrics, for example, if you put the machine on left (preferably) or right needle position, then three-quarters of the needle will be surrounded by the rim of the hole. The fabric won't get poked down in and become pulled or frayed. Don't forget, however, that when you change needle position, you have also changed the placement of your 5/8" seam-allowance guide.

Note: If your machine doesn't have a single-hole needle plate, you may want to tape the opening with opaque Scotch tape to prevent fine fabrics from being pushed down in with the needle.

If you don't have a needle position on your machine, you will have trouble adjusting for many of the alternate presser feet. For example, the needle must be in the exact position to get a good hem with the rolled hem foot. If your needle is just 1/16" off, you won't get the stitching line down the center of the roll, and the hem will not work.

Pressure Regulator

Not all machines have a pressure regulator or adjustment dial. They are more common on older machines. The dial was invented to help thicker fabric move between the feed dogs and the foot by creating more space. This adjustment changed the pressure on the foot for different weights of fabrics.

Now most machines are spring-loaded, so the pressure regulator is obsolete. Most often you will want the pressure on the fabric to be as tight as possible, so it is better to change feet to lighten the pressure. Adjusting the pressure regulator can increase the risks of flutter and skipped stitches.

Note: If your machine isn't feeding properly, check that your pressure regulator is engaged. Also check your sew/darn lever, if your machine has one.

Tension Mechanism

By now, you understand that tension is resistance against the thread as

it travels through the machine. It is not only that little knob or dial on the front or top of the machine that you turn to adjust the setting. This statement bears repeating, because not understanding this fact is a mind-set that creates most home-sewing problems.

What we refer to as "tension" is basically two things: (1) Where do the knots fall in the fabric? (2) Is the seam puckered? (Remember, if the thread is thicker than the fabric, you will see the knots protruding slightly on both sides.) If either of these two variables is improper, we usually call it "tension problems." But the real problem is usually a multitude of layers. **The least of our problems is usually that knob.**

I have discussed the upper tension mechanism in describing the thread's path through the machine. The bottom mechanism is not as strong as the top because its only function is to anchor the thread firmly enough so the top thread can loop over to form the knot or stitch. The top thread has a longer path to the knot, and so has a wider variable more critical to stitch formation.

There are reasons and uses for changing both upper and lower tension mechanisms to get the machine to work to your advantage.

On certain machines, you can loosen the upper mechanism for smoother long stitch lengths. Because there is less resistance, the fabric can then move forward without pulling up and developing puckers.

When you work on lightweight fabrics, such as silk, you might try loosening the upper and lower mechanisms equally. The knots will still form in the middle, but there won't be so much pull against the thread to cause puckers. Finer fabrics have difficulty stabilizing the stitches, as stated, so this is one way to reduce the tug of war between the threads.

If you loosen only the upper tension mechanism, the knots fall to the bottom. In reality, that's better than puckers, but the seam will be weak. If the two mechanisms are loosened equally, the knots are stronger and will not pull out as easily.

Basting

When you baste, loosen the upper tension mechanism by about half the normal. Also up the stitch length all the way. This procedure allows the knots to fall to the bottom, and the lower thread will pull out more easily when you've finished. Also, you won't get puckers, even with the long stitch.

Although there is no danger to the machine in loosening this mechanism, if you loosen it too much, you can cause a jam underneath; there will be no resistance on the thread to pull it back up again. If you must loosen the tension, do so in small increments, only until the knots fall to the bottom.

Gathering

To machine-gather, tighten the upper tension mechanism so the knots come to the top of the fabric. The feed dogs still push the fabric, but the thread isn't giving at all. The material then bunches up as you sew along.

Another gathering technique, called finger-easing, is to put your left or right index finger gently behind the presser foot as you sew. That action will cause the material to pleat up slightly, so the thread doesn't have space to spread itself to form a complete stitch. Instead, it gathers the material. This technique is especially good for bias or corners.

If you have a pre–World War II machine, however, do not crank the tension knob up and down all the time to baste or gather, unless your manual recommends it. You can permanently compress the spring that regulates the tension in that assembly, throwing it off. If you have had problems with varying tensions on that mechanism, know that the knob should not be adjusted. In some cases a repair person can untighten the spring, but that's costly. Preventive maintenance is always best.

The tension mechanism should not have to be adjusted to accommodate multiple layers, since they are more stabilizing for the threads. The machine will automatically pull down more thread for a proper stitch.

As for the bottom mechanism, if you plan to adjust it often (for example, for machine embroidery or silk), please buy another bobbin case. Overadjusting the set screw can eventually loosen it so much that it will no longer hold any tension. Mark the extra bobbin case with a spot of nail polish.

Zigzag Stitch

Let's start by describing how the zigzag stitch is formed. You usually zigzag on your machine's widest width and on medium length; let's use a width of 4 and a length of 2 for now. If the machine is then set up to pull down a maximum of 4 mm of thread and you also want it to move 2 mm forward, then you are asking that it pull down 6 mm of thread to cover a 4 mm space. So you get puckers—that all-too-familiar tunnel down the center that says to everyone, "Hi, I made me." In fact, these ironed ridges are among the worst tell-tale signs of homemade clothing. They can be avoided.

Put the edge of the fabric under the center of the foot. By doing this, the needle will zag off the edge, but you will be using only 2 mm of thread instead of 4 mm across, equaling 4 mm total thread for 4 mm of distance. Your seam allowance won't pucker, and the edges won't pull up (Fig. 4.17). Best of all, no tunnels; the seam allowances will lie flat.

I believe that a zigzag should be used only for satin stitching, button-holes, and appliqué. When you sew these projects, be sure to stabilize the area beneath with something like Stitch 'n' Tear. When the material is firm enough, the machine will automatically pull down another little length of thread to match the resistance of the fabric, so you elim-inate tunneling.

The zigzag is also wonderful for making any long, straight seam, partic-ularly on drapery or bias fabrics. You may have noticed that if you used a straight stitch on a round or A-line skirt, for instance, the seam appeared flat when laying on a surface. Yet it pulled up when the garment was hung or worn. This is because it had no give; the seam was stabilized into one straight line. If instead you use a small zigzag, a width of 1 and length of 1 1/2 or "fine," this seam will hang out the fabric and the sides won't pull up shorter or pucker. The seam will still press open as well.

If you thought this problem was caused by "the tension," now you know better. It was caused by the way the seam was formed.

This small zigzag also works well to form seams with knits if you don't

Fig. 4.17

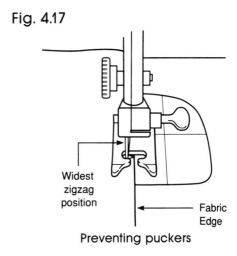

Widest zigzag position — Fabric Edge

Preventing puckers

Fig. 4.18

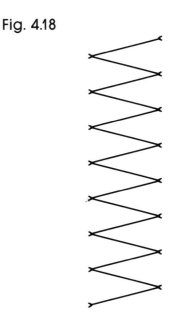

Properly adjusted zigzag (from wrong side)

own an overlock, or if you just want to join an area on wool jersey, on circles, or wovens cut on the bias, for example.

Don't forget that the spongier or thicker the fabric, the more slowly it will move through your machine. You may need to increase your stitch length slightly on zigzag so that the seam hangs well.

Note: Repairmen always test the tension of any machine on zigzag. You can also do this. If you set it at its widest width and normal length (2 1/2 or 15/inch), then when you turn the material over you should see small loops on the bottom (Fig. 4.18). This is *correct.* The knots should not meet in the middle on zigzag because then they would come up to the top when the machine was reset for straight stitch. You need that extra pull on the upper thread—more tension—so that it can pull itself up after circling the bobbin casing.

Also note that if you are getting skipped stitches on your zigzag, your machine might be out of time. If so, it means the hook is barely picking up the first knot and missing the second one altogether. Skips on the left can also mean a needle problem (burr, wrong

Fig. 4.19

Serpentine stitch

size), while varying skips can indicate improper or poor-quality thread.

▶ For all those times when it seems that no matter what you do you still get puckers, completely rethread the machine. Then try a test sample on the actual fabric, with correct thread, needle, and foot, and see if that makes a difference.

Serpentine Stitch

Most machines now feature an alternate stitch called the serpentine (multiple zigzag or running) stitch (Fig. 4.19). I consider it the most underrated stitch in the world because almost no when pressed, puts the feed dogs into reverse. If you depress the mechanism completely, this action makes a long stitch and results in puckers. If you don't depress the lever to its maximum, you will have a shorter stitch length and fewer chances of puckering.

Reverse-Cycle Stitches

The other way that the machine sews in reverse is with a special reverse cycle or stretch stitches.

Unless you are careful, these stitches will also pucker. They are *not* formed like overlock stitches, no matter what you have heard. The home machine has a bobbin, whereas the overlock a looper. Never will the stitches be identical.

Some machines have "straight stretch stitches," which is a misnomer: they don't have much stretch. The cycle is usually some combination of two stitches forward, one back. They are an extremely good combination of two stitches, especially in high-stress areas: they will not rip out. For a wonderful repair stitch, set the width at zero. But on anything less than bulletproof polyester or very firm fabric such as denim, the fabric will usually pucker.

Since these stitches are virtually impossible to rip out, first sew the seam with the normal stitch to test for accuracy. Then go over it with the stretch stitch for reinforcement.

two ways, and both have a proper technique.

Your machine probably has some kind of reverse button or lever that,

5

GREMMIE AWARDS

Just when you thought it was safe to start sewing again, "the machine" acts up. It's what I call "gremmies"—all the crunches, crashes, and whirs that drive you crazy as you're sewing along. Whenever you hear yourself scream "What now?"—that's a gremmie. Gremmies are those things that go wrong and you don't know why, problems you thought were your machine but are in fact "operator" problems. In other words, it's *your* fault, whether from mind-set or oversight.

Gremmie 1 is a kerplunk at the beginning of your sewing. You may have the bad habit of threading your machine with the presser-foot lifter down. This is the bar that lifts up the foot or sets it onto the feed dogs. When the bar is up, the tension mechanism's separating plates are disengaged, so there is no tension or resistance against the thread. Conversely, when the presser lifter is down, the tension is engaged.

If you thread your machine with the lifter down, the upper thread won't be set securely between the plates. There will be no tension on the thread, and you will find a small wad underneath, causing a jam.

If you do monogramming or darning that requires no foot, you still must lower the presser-foot lifter to engage the tension. Otherwise you will have wads, jams, and thread breakage underneath.

When working on thick fabrics, you may be able to prevent this gremmie by hand-walking the fabric through the machine.

There are actually two kinds of jams: Gremmie 1 occurs under the fabric. Gremmie 2 occurs underneath in the bobbin area. Check closely to see which one is your problem.

Gremmie 2 is the jam when you first start sewing and get a wad underneath. If you don't hold onto the threads when you first sew, the slack can get caught and hang up underneath. Do not tug at the threads; just hold them gently to the back and start slowly. This technique also helps the fabric feed for those first stitches.

Gremmie 3 is a jam that you can hear coming. It means the thread has wrapped around the bobbin case. Your manual will tell you in which direction the thread passes through the casing. The direction is not the same on all machines. When you place the thread in the casing, be sure you hear the little click that means it is securely in the tension disk. Otherwise the thread can pull out and cause jams.

There is an important technique to picking up that first bobbin thread.

Most of us were taught to hold onto the upper thread and pull it until the bobbin thread came up and the machine made its first stitch.

But because you now know that at the beginning and ending of each stitch the uptake is at its highest point, if you will then place one finger on the upper thread against the throat plate and make one complete stitch with the handwheel (or single stitch button, if available), the bobbin thread will always come up easily. You then will not get a jam caused by a thread's wrapping around the outside of the bobbin casing.

If you do get a jam, rock the handwheel back and forth sharply. The hook will act like a knife and loosen just about anything jammed in there. You can't throw the machine out of time by doing this; it takes more strength than you can generate with your hand. The thread will break before any metal part will.

Gremmie 4 is thread breaking when you first start to sew. If you have the habit of backing the handwheel to remove the needle from the fabric, you are going to break threads. When you back out, you create an extra loop of thread at the uptake, which will snap and break when you start sewing again. The handwheel is meant to turn in one direction only: **forward.**

As well, be sure the thread isn't

coming loose from the spindle and wrapping around it. This can cause broken threads.

Gremmie 5 is skipped stitches and broken threads. This is your clue that the needle may be inserted incorrectly. It must be all the way up inside the needle clamp screw, and firmly tightened. It also must be inserted with the flat section facing the proper direction. In most machines it faces the back, but check your manual if you aren't sure.

Gremmie 6 is when you are sewing along and in the middle you hear a klunk. Usually you find a ball of thread below. This gremmie is the improperly wound bobbin, which will cause many problems. If it has loose spots, it will pull too easily from the case and jam underneath. If it is wound too tightly, it will break suddenly while you're sewing. And if it is overfilled—that is, if you have to jam it into the casing—it will create more drag on the thread, adding resistance in the form of those gram weights by which tension is measured. In short, it will throw your tension out of whack. (See Chapter 4, under *Bobbins.*)

Gremmie 7 is when the needle breaks as you're sewing. Chances are, you were tugging at the fabric from the back to "help" the machine feed. If you pull when the needle enters the fabric, it can bend back, strike the throat plate,

and break or cause burrs. If you need to firm the fabric, fine—just don't yank on it. A repair person can always recognize a "fabric puller" by all the little nicks behind the throat-plate hole.

Gremmie 8 is when your stitches are wobbly and uneven. Check your pressure regulator. If it is not pressing firmly enough, the fabric will shift under the foot instead of progressing smoothly forward. If this change doesn't work, check your needle point. Is it too round for your fabric? Reread Chapter 3.

Gremmie 9 is when you hear a clank and your needle breaks. Have you sewn over pins? Anyone who ever told you that you could lied to you. No machine was truly made to sew over pins. *Remember:* **When two pieces of metal come together, one is going to lose.** It's generally the needle, because that's the piece that's moving. But whichever one gives, it's hard on the machine (and hard on the needle, even if it doesn't break). Pins must be removed *before* they reach the foot. No exceptions.

Gremmie 10 is when you have loops on either the top or bottom of the seam. I know you want one of those little drawings that tell you to make one adjustment if the loops are up here and another if they fall down there. **Adjusting the tension mechanism is the court of last resort.** Once you have checked *everything else,* then and only then should you reach to adjust the tension knob or dial.

It can be said that if the knot loops are on the botton, most likely the upper tension is too loose. Or if they are on top, the bottom tension is too loose. **But there are no absolutes.** The top could be too tight, pulling up the knots, and vice versa. The telltale sign of either being too tight is extreme puckering.

The object is to create a balance between upper and lower tensions. Because the top mechanism is easier to deal with, adjust it first while the machine is sewing a scrap of material. Watch the seam, and see if the adjustment makes a difference in where the knots meet. Make all adjustments in small increments.

Gremmie 11 is when you are sewing up to a jeans seam and your machine won't go over the lump, or if it does, the needle breaks. Cure this by using a shim to create an even height for the foot to press on. I use a business card or matchcover folded in thirds. Put the needle into the fabric and raise the presser foot. Slide the folded card in from the back until it rests against the needle. Put the presser foot down and sew over the lump (see Fig. 4.15).

Gremmie 12 is when you've tried everything. The machine won't work, and you still don't know why. In this case, unthread the *entire* machine, change the needle (even if it's brand new), and rethread carefully. In my own sewing, sometimes this simple procedure cures a problem that seems to have no cause. Sometimes, you may never know why a problem occurs, even though you can fix it.

Gremmie 13 is when you can't seem to sew straight seams with consistent seam allowance width. If this happens, you are a needle watcher. The up-and-down motion of the needle mesmerizes the eyes. Train your eye to look only at the fabric edge and its alignment to the width marks on the throat plate or the foot edge in relation to a line on the fabric.

Remember: Commercial machines are not like home machines; they do one function very well. Although home machines are more versatile, they cannot reproduce commercial stitches. Be realistic—personally constructed garments cannot look exactly like the ones you buy. But they can be beautiful, professional, and unique, your own creative expression. They don't have to look homemade.

PART II
SERGERS (OVERLOCKS)

RULES OF READING

The differences and similarities between your traditional sewing machine and a serger (overlock) are more than how they look, how many threads they use, or that they both are used on sewing projects. This confusion of not understanding is the cause of many of your frustrations.

But you have one up on most people if you have read and studied Part I. The better you understand traditional sewing machines, the more apparent the differences and similarities to overlocks will be. Understanding can only be built on accurate knowledge.

Again, I ask you to keep on reading, even if things seem unclear. This is not a how-to book but a *WHY?* book. It takes longer to learn why, but it is more valuable in the long run.

As in Part I, I want you to read the manual that came with your overlock. Though I would be the first to admit that the manuals provided by the manufacturers are not the best, I highly recommend you read it. Replace it if you don't have one. Read it from cover to cover once a year.

As you read, please note where the following items are positioned on your machine so that you will recognize them as they appear later:

1. Handwheel
2. Tension mechanisms (one per thread)

3. Check spring(s) on one or more tension mechanisms (optional)
4. Stitch width mechanism or alternate throat plates
5. Stitch length selector
6. Presser foot lifter
7. Presser foot adjuster or pressure regulator (often not named or noted)
8. Feed dogs
9. Differential feed adjuster (optional)
10. Fixed cutter
11. Movable cutter
12. Needle(s)
13. Needle clamp screw(s)
14. Lower looper
15. Upper looper
16. Thread guide pole
17. Thread caps and/or nets
18. Cone stabilizers
19. Looper threader (optional)
20. Tweezers (necessity)

All machines feature most of these parts, but they may be located in slightly different areas, look different, or have different names. As with sewing machines, one illustration can't cover all variations, and there isn't room here to draw them all. If your manual has a photo or drawing, look at it. Better yet, photocopy it and attach it to this page. The manual of your brand may not note the placement of all these parts, but each machine has its version of these parts. I am trusting you to do your part in this learning process.

6

WHAT OVERLOCKS REALLY DO

The terms "overlock" and "serger" will be used interchangeably throughout this book. Originally, the commercial machine devised to finish edges rapidly was called a serger. The stitches locked the edges of the fabric with thread to prevent raveling and this became known as an overlock stitch. By the time these machines were introduced to the home sewing market, the words "serger" and "overlock" had become synonymous.

If you look at an overlock and feel overwhelmed, you are not alone. They do look very different from traditional machines, with so many knobs, dials, threads, and other parts that seem confusing. Yet the serger is easier to use than a traditional sewing machine, once you get the hang of it.

Overlocks are the greatest boon to home sewers since electricity. They have cut my sewing time in half. My garments are now ravel-free and professionally finished. And they make sewing on knit fabrics a breeze.

What sergers do, they do very well, but they do have limitations. Contrary to what you might hear, a serger will not replace a traditional machine.

The overlock will speed up your sewing. It overcasts edges probably three times faster than doing a similar edge on a traditional machine, and it does a better job of it.

Stitch Formation

Both sergers and sewing machines use thread to join together pieces of fabric, but that is where the similarity ends.

An overlock creates a stitch more like crocheting or knitting than what is normally termed "sewing." Two of the threads loop back and forth on the top and bottom of the fabric. These threads are captured by another thread to form a soft but stable overcast (Fig. 6.1). If you can visualize the formation of a stitch, you will begin to understand how a serger works.

The thread that moves under the fabric is called the lower looper. Because it's hard to see, the lower looper can be difficult to thread. The upper looper is the thread that comes up over the fabric.

The serger's biggest limitation is assembling woven fabrics. A traditional

Fig. 6.1

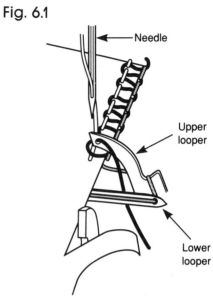

How a serger forms a stitch

machine forms a knot within the fabric that anchors the seam together. With the stitch formed by a serger on woven fabrics, you can see the loose thread on the seam on the *right* side (Fig. 6.2). Even if you tighten the needle tension until the seam puckers or the thread breaks, the seam will still look as if the tension is off. Sergers that have a chain stitch (safety or locking chain) will make a neater seam, but never exactly like a traditional seam.

Knit fabrics, on the other hand, because of the loft and stretch of their construction, fill in the spaces between the threads. So you can make accept-

Fig. 6.2

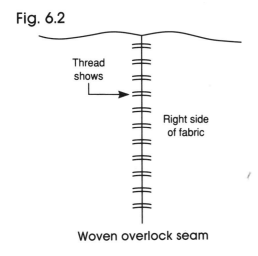

Thread shows →

Right side of fabric

Woven overlock seam

Fig. 6.3

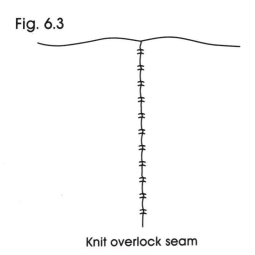

Knit overlock seam

able-looking seams on a serger that are less bulky and have more stretch (Fig. 6.3).

I believe the unrealistic expecta-tions of what sergers can do have caused many people to become disgruntled with their machines when they should be cheering. Read on and learn to love your serger.

Two Important Facts About Sergers

When people complain about overlocks, they usually complain about a recurrent jam. I often hear this: "I've used an overlock, but it drives me crazy. When I change thread, I can't get the tension back in adjustment." My reply is "I can cure all your problems by ex-plaining two simple facts."

Fact #1—When you lift up the presser foot on your traditional sewing machine, it releases the separating plates on the tension mechanism, so that you can pull the thread free. When the sep-arating plates are not engaged, there is no pressure on the thread. *That never happens on an overlock.* They never open.

This seems like a trivial fact, but it is not. **It is one of the two most im-portant and least understood facets of using your serger.** Because the sepa-rating plates are not open unless the tension has been turned off (down to 0), the thread does not get inside where the pressure can control the thread.

Some home sewers thread an overlock in the same way as a traditional sewing machine. They just guide the thread around the tension mechanism. Unfortunately, the thread sits around the edge without being held between the plates. Remember that the plates are closed unless the tension is turned off.

So if you are working on your serger and it seems you have no tension for no reason, check to see if the thread is truly where it belongs. On the other hand, you may be right; you may not have tension.

If your stitches don't look right, immediately check that the thread is in between the separating plates. To make sure the thread is inside the tension mechanism, you must either turn the mechanism to zero while threading or pull the thread into the slot by holding onto it with both hands and tugging lightly. Next, check that the thread is in all the little thread guides, called escapements.

Fact #2—An overlock makes a stitch in a completely different way than a traditional machine. Overlocks function *sequentially*, and the complicated order of stitch formation must be followed exactly in a precise order. So, to form stitches, without exception:

You must thread the needle last

That means if one of your loopers breaks, you have to clip the threads right above the eye of the needle. You don't have to take the thread out of the machine, but you do have to pull it out of the eye of the needle. This knowledge will save you hours and hours of frustration.

Obviously no one in her right mind wants to rethread the eye of the needle any more times than absolutely necessary. I know that many people will try to get around this—but don't try it! If the thread is in the eye of the needle and you don't thread the rest of the serger perfectly, you will end up with a knot instead of a chain.

You cannot tell the beginning of a chain from the beginning of a knot. It helps to start your chain by turning the handwheel by hand for the first few stitches.

This information is in the manuals, but it may be hidden among other, not-so-important information. You must be conscious of these two facts every single time you approach your serger.

Proofing the Threading

When beginning to thread an overlock from scratch, start with the lower looper. Next thread the upper looper.

When you have the loopers threaded, you must proof the looper paths before you do anything with the needles. To proof the loopers, put your thumb or finger over the threads that you have guided to the back under the foot (Fig. 6.4). Make three complete revolutions of the handwheel. The needle will catch the thread as it descends. As the needle goes up again, it wil completely release the threads.

If you thread the overlock wrong, the threads become tangled on or around the loopers or needles. It makes no difference where it happens. It's the beginning of a problem. Yet if the thread were in the needle, it would look to you like the beginning of the usual chain.

A most frustrating aspect of these machines is that problems rarely show up when they occur. They usually show up an inch or so later. About 1" into a seam, the machine starts to make a raspy noise; then the thread breaks. Unless you unthread the needles and proof the thread path before continuing, this will happen over and over until you go crazy. So when this happens, don't fool with it; just proof it. **Now and only now do you thread the needles**.

One of the differences between a traditional sewing machine and an overlock is what happens to the thread when the seam ends. A sewing machine

Fig. 6.4

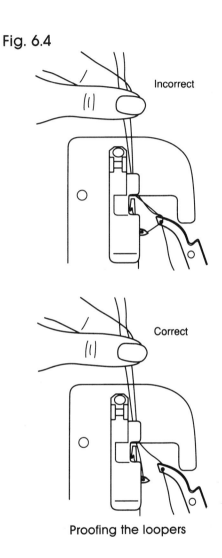

Proofing the loopers

stops and the thread simply pulls free. On a serger, as you sew off the end of the fabric, you must continue sewing, leaving a little tail of thread that resembles a chain; hence, the term "chaining off."

Stitch Width

The width of the stitch of an overlock is determined by the size of the finger over which the stitch is made (Fig. 6.5). On a sewing machine, the needle swings back and forth. The distance of the movement creates different widths. On a serger, the needle doesn't swing. The stitch finger over which the looper moves and forms the stitch decides the width. The stitch finger is a small prong that sits immediately to the right of the needle. The loopers arc over and under the finger, and then the thread and fabric slide off the back of the prong.

The different brands and models of sergers have a variety of methods for changing the stitch width. Some have a different plate for each width. Others have a movable projection that is held in place by screws, knobs, dials, or sliders. Each type has advantages and drawbacks. The changeable plates take extra storage and changing space, but they are very secure. The movable type is speedy to change, but isn't as foolproof.

No matter how the overcast stitch is formed, it remains exactly as wide as

Fig. 6.5

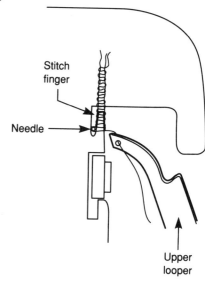

Stitch finger determines chain width

the width of the finger over which it is formed.

Tension

Prepare to adjust the tensions on your serger more than you do on your sewing machine. On your traditional machine, you have two mechanisms that control the amount of thread the machine feeds out: an uptake (the thing that goes up and down) and the bobbin. An overlock doesn't have either of these mechanisms. Therefore, you have to account for all the vagaries in fabric and thread by adjusting the tension mechanisms.

> *Note:* If a big slub comes off the spool and hits the tension wrong, it will slide around the dial and pull the thread out of the separating plates instead of through it. This is why the tension occasionally goes haywire in mid-seam.

Cutting Blades

A serger also functions as a cutter. It can either shear away pieces of fabric and seam allowances or simply trim away the fuzzy edges.

An overlock has two cutters (Fig. 6.6). One is the movable cutter, which can come from above the machine surface or from below. This blade moves up and down with each stitch the machine makes. The other is a fixed (stationary) cutter that the movable blade rubs against. These blades slice against each other to cut. The movable cutter is made of a softer metal than the fixed cutter and can be replaced when it gets dull.

Fig. 6.6

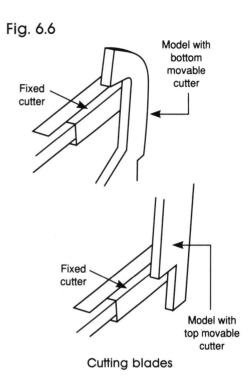

Cutting blades

Rolled Hem

One of the advantages of a serger is the ability to do narrow satin-stitched edges fast. This edge can be used on many items, from table linens to fancy ruffles.

To achieve a narrow overcast, you must change the width of the stitch finger by adjusting or by changing the plate

Fig. 6.7

Unchanged tension   Very tight tension

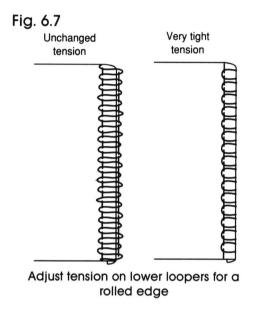

Adjust tension on lower loopers for a rolled edge

Fig. 6.8

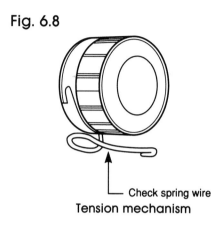

Check spring wire
Tension mechanism

(Fig. 6.7). To make a smooth narrow edge, the tension on the loopers must be increased to double, triple, or even more.

Check Springs

Check springs, found on some overlocks, are small wires that come from the tension mechanism (Fig. 6.8). Not all brands use them, but be sure to check your machine and *read your manual.* The spring adds additional tension on the thread. Some sergers always use them and others use them only to increase the tension when the width is decreased.

Hint: If you can't get the tension tight enough, loop the thread around the tension mechanism twice.

This chapter has laid the foundation for your journey to successful overlocking. Keep these basic functions and facts in mind as you continue to learn and understand your serger.

7

OVERLOCK CHOICES AND OPTIONS

The choices among models and options on sergers are complex. The obvious choice would seem to be the one that does the most. Unfortunately, sergers are not that simple.

Each type and each brand has its own set of strong points and problems. A good method for deciding which will be best for you is to make a list of all the possible ways you can foresee utilizing a serger. Then give priority to the options you will need the most.

Here is a list of the most common choices and a few of their attributes:

▶ Three-thread machines. This basic overlock has two looper threads with a single needle thread that holds the looper threads in place (Fig. 7.1). The width of the stitch can range from the narrowest rolled hem of 1.5 mm to the widest overcast at 5 mm, the stretchiest of all the configurations.

Fig. 7.1

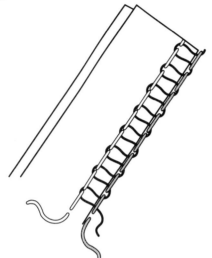

3-thread overlock

Fig. 7.2

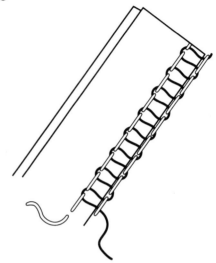

2-thread overlock

▶ Three/two-thread machine. This model can do the same stitch as the standard three-thread, but it has the option of creating a fine soft edge of only two threads (Fig. 7.2). This is recommended for silk and other fine fabrics. Unfortunately, the mechanism for switching off the upper looper can make the machine very temperamental.

▶ Three/four-thread machine. This overlock can add an extra needle and thread along the center of the normal overcast stitch (Fig. 7.3). This thread acts as a stabilizer for extremely ravelly fabrics like hand-wovens and mohair. Also use it when you need to decrease stretch. The medium and widest width changes can be made easily by threading the other needle.

Fig. 7.3

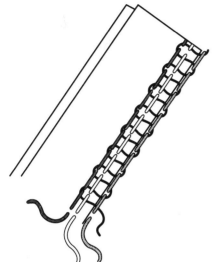

3/4-thread overlock

Fig. 7.4

Forms chain stitch
on reverse

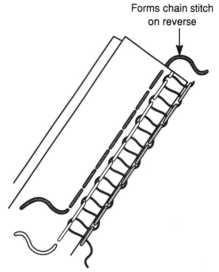

4-thread overlock

▶ Four-thread. This serger has the 3-thread edge with the addition of a chain-stitch seam 1/4″ to the left of the overcast needle thread (Fig. 7.4). The biggest drawback on these models is the awkward way they maneuver around corners when the chain is being used. The chain can only be used on the gentlest of inside curves without jamming or sewing off the edge.

▶ Five-thread. Most of these sergers can use two, three, four, or five threads at a time, the widest variety of options. At first glance, this seems like your best choice, but it is also the most complicated. For many home sewers these overlocks are so intricate that the struggle and time spent to learn and use them makes them inefficient.

Note: When threading the seam needle on a 5-thread machine, the first few stitches must be turned by hand with the needle entering a scrap of fabric to prevent tangles and breaks. If it enters air only, you may have trouble.

Needles

There are almost as many needle types as there are brands of overlocks. Some machines require special serger needles that are round on the top. They have no flat side to hold the needle in alignment. The many varieties of serger needles have their own specification of overall length and the depth of the scarf. They are usually classified by letters such as DC or BL. Check your manual for which one exactly fits your machine.

Note: If your machine uses a round upper-shank serger needle, you may have a difficult time aligning the eye straight to the front. After placing the needles in their approximate location, put a toothpick or bamboo skewer in the eye and you will be able to see if it is facing forward (Fig. 7.5).

Fig. 7.5

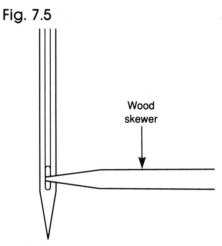

Wood skewer

Straightening needle to exact front

Some overlocks can use traditional sewing machine needles, but even these needles have their idiosyncrasies. The European needles have a deeper scarf on the back (see needle information in Part I) and cause skips on machines set up for inexpensive Asian needles. If you use a traditional needle without the indentation on a machine set up for a scarf needle, it will come too close to the looper and could nick it.

Even within the same needle brand, changes have occurred over the years. When buying needles, have your date of purchase and serial number of your serger with you to make sure you buy the right needle.

You will be delighted to know I am not going to nag you about changing your needle every time you use it. Be-

Fig. 7.6

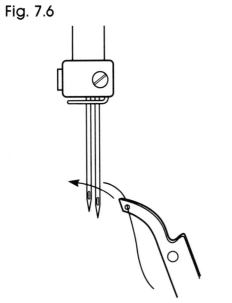

Righthand needle is lower, due to arc

look wrong to you, but they are in the correct configuration. Check your manual to be sure that the right needle is supposed to be lower than the left on a 2-thread serger. The height difference is due to the rising arc of the upper looper as it comes up and over the fabric.

Overlocks handle knit fabric with ease. They rarely skip stitches, no matter how tricky the fabric. This is a good thing because ballpoint needles should not be used on sergers. The full round tip can graze and damage a looper.

cause the serger thread doesn't slide back and forth through the eye of the needle, you can use it for eight to ten garments before changing the needle. Even so, if the overlock begins to skip, first try changing the needle.

The size of the needle is also not as crucial in an overlock as it is in a traditional machine. The majority of your sewing can be done with a 75/11 or 80/12, a rare 60/8 (remember to use fine thread), and an even rarer 90/14 for heavy fabrics.

On a machine with two or more needles, the needles are set at slightly different heights (Fig. 7.6). This may

Stitch-Length Settings

The stitch length of a standard overcast is usually given in millimeters between stitches, one (1) being the shortest and five (5) being the longest. Three (3) is the average and the setting most often used. The shortest stitch length would create a satin stitch much like a traditional machine. Some sergers don't have a numbered stitch-length dial, which makes them difficult to adjust accurately.

If you were working on an extremely thick or spongy piece of fabric, you might need a different stitch length. Don't forget, even though you set a stitch

Fig. 7.7

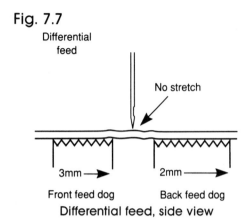

Differential feed

No stretch

3mm →   2mm →

Front feed dog   Back feed dog

Differential feed, side view

feed." These sergers have two sets of feed dogs that function independently of each other. One set is toward the front of the foot and one set is near the back. By adjusting the rate of movement, the rear set spits the fabric out the back slower than the front pulls it into the machine (Fig. 7.7). The differential feed reduces the stretch and distortion of the fabric, which is important on many knits.

length, you are really only setting the amount of push the feed dogs will exert on the fabric. A thick piece of fabric may have difficulty traveling under the foot. Even though the feed dogs push with the same force as on a thinner piece, they can't move the thick fabric quite as well. It's like driving your car. You push the gas pedal down to a certain level to go 35 mph on a flat road, but as you go uphill, you will drop back to 20 mph if you don't increase the gas. Likewise, overlocks require a longer or shorter length setting to achieve the same measured distance.

Pressure Regulator

The pressure regulator is on the top left portion of the machine. This screw adjusts the amount of push the foot exerts on the fabric. Unfortunately, most manuals don't even name this crucial part, let alone give you instructions for its use. This adjuster, when properly used, makes the differential feed almost unnecessary.

When the foot presses hard on certain types of fabric, like sweater knits, the fabric will flatten out of shape. Then the machine stay-stitches the stretched edge in place. The overlocked edge will be wavy and permanently out of shape (Fig. 7.8).

Differential Feed

In addition to needles and numbers of threads, you must consider an optional feature called "differential

If you keep turning the presser foot adjuster to the left (counterclockwise), the knob will actually fall off in your hand. Put it back on the serger and give

Fig. 7.8

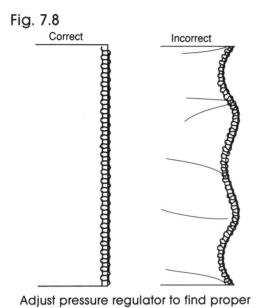

Correct   Incorrect

Adjust pressure regulator to find proper setting

it one full turn to the right. This setting exerts the minimum amount of pressure on the fabric needed to create a stitch. This is the setting for soft, squishy, and stretchy fabrics. If you were working on a sweater knit, this minimum setting would be the correct pressure setting.

As you turn the knob to the right, the pressure increases on the fabric. The thinner or slicker the fabric, the more push the foot needs to exert on the fabric to keep it from wiggling.

Take the time to practice and experiment with this vital adjustment. Once you master the proper setting for your projects, your overcast edges will be perfect.

Specialized Feet

Several specialized feet come with a serger or are available as options:

1. Rolled Hem Foot—Many sergers require a specific foot to do a tiny rolled hem. These feet hold the fabric firmly to obtain the best stitch.
2. Elastic Application Foot—Several brands make a special foot for the application of elastic on the very edge of the fabric (Fig. 7.9). These feet have a screw on the top to regulate the degree of pucker. For example, you want more pucker under the seat on a leotard compared to the front of the leg.
3. Stabilizer Guide Foot—This foot has holes through it that act as a guide for sewing cord or twill tape under or into the serger seam (Fig. 7.10). This foot is a standard feature on some machines. On others it can be purchased separately (see your dealer).
4. Swing-Away Foot—This foot helps make the threading easier. The ability to fit your finger close to the needle really helps.

Fig. 7.9

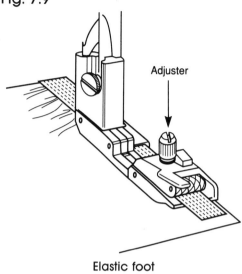

Elastic foot

Fig. 7.10

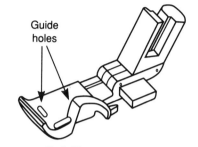

Stabilizer guide foot

Fig. 7.11

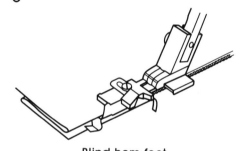

Blind-hem foot

5. Blind-Hem Foot—The serger does a very good blind hem on knits. The hem of knit tops sewn on a traditional sewing machine or by hand will usually break when stretched. The overlock creates a soft stretchable hem that holds up very well on knit fabrics. The foot made for blind hemming serves the same function as a blind-hem foot on a traditional sewing machine (Fig. 7.11). It has an adjustable guide that slides against the same type of blind-hem fold.

Unfortunately the serger blind hem is not acceptable on woven fabric. The stitches are too close together and have too many threads to be invisible. Stick to your traditional methods on wovens.

Optional Attachments

In addition to feet, several other optional attachments are available:

1. Containers for the Trimmings— Because of the cutting action of

Fig. 7.12

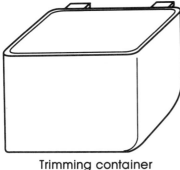

Trimming container

Fig. 7.13

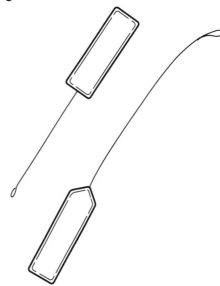

Looper and needle threaders

the serger, there seems to be a never-ending trail of fabric, threads, and fuzz. To catch these droppings, baskets, cups, or boxes are available, depending on your brand or model. Some machines come with these containers attached and others can be purchased separately (Fig. 7.12).

If you have had your serger for a while, contact your dealer. Several brands now have this feature as an add-on item.

2. Threaders—The lower looper is especially difficult to thread. Several brands come with a threader, but most are not very durable. Check with your dealer or look in a sewing notion catalogue for new, longer, stronger, thinner threaders. These have a fine loop on the end and a very long wire to feed easily through the machine (Fig. 7.13).

3. Thread Guides—When you want to use a special fiber or a stabilizer thread, a separate thread stand is helpful. The stand has a tall pole that holds and guides or a clip that is attached to the standard pole as an extra thread guide (Fig. 7.14).

4. Thread Nets—These small flexible plastic nets keep slippery thread feeding evenly off the cone or spool (Fig. 7.15). The net fits over the entire cone and the thread comes easily out of the top.

Fig. 7.14

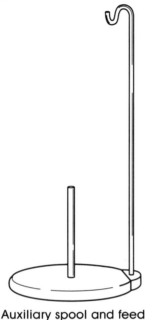

Auxiliary spool and feed

Fig. 7.15

Plastic net allows thread to feed evenly
off spool

Set Screws

Many overlocks have set screws for adjusting the cutting-blade position and stitch width. A pair of set screws anchors a shaft that passes throughout the machine to keep it from sliding or rotating by piercing it along the side. You will see them as a set of two identical screws close together. Loosen them both before making any changes.

When inserting the set screws, tighten one side slightly, then the other, alternating until they are both snug. If you completely tighten one side, then the other, it will wedge the shaft in crooked, possibly jamming the whole machine.

Looper Threaders

On most overlock brands, the lower looper is the most difficult to thread. Many of them come with a special looper threader (Fig. 7.16). Because of the tiny hole they must slide through, the threaders are made of fine wire and break easily. If you find one that works for you, buy several. I get better results

Fig. 7.16

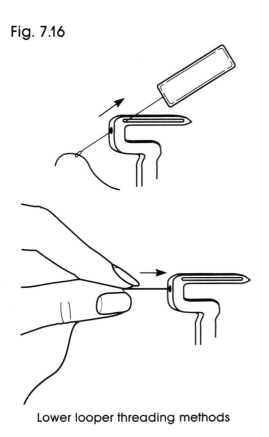

Lower looper threading methods

can work its way out of the loopers with this type of guide and you may get a jam. If the problem is severe, it can be adjusted. Check with your dealer.

Tools

Screwdrivers

Two screwdrivers are generally included with your attachments. The primary use of the large screwdriver is to change the throat plate. Some brands also use a big screwdriver for adusting the fixed cutter position, stitch length, and other adjustments.

▶ Screwdrivers are meant to be used with two hands. You push down with one hand and rotate with the other. That way you won't scab the top of the screws. See Fig. 2.2.

Use the small screwdriver to change the needles. The needle screws should be barely loosened while holding onto the needles. The needles drop out easily and tend to fall inside the machine when not grasped firmly. If there are two needles, don't loosen the needle clamp screw too far or it will be difficult to feel the groove inside the needle shaft.

by stuffing the thread through the hole in the end of the looper and catching it on the other side with the tweezers.

Look for the snap-in thread guides. Insert thread as if you were flossing teeth: hold thread on either side and snap into the snap-in guide. These thread carriers are excellent on fixed and minimally moving areas. When the machine is moving rapidly, the thread

Tweezers

Tweezers will rapidly become your best friend when working on an overlock. I use them when threading the needle as well as the looper. I own several tweezers and keep one inside the body of the machine for easy accessibility. Tweezers must come together cleanly at the tips and have no snags. Smooth the tips of your tweezers regularly by rubbing them with crocus cloth.

8

WICKS, FUZZ, AND OTHER DIRTY MATTERS

Oiling Your Serger

A serger's need for oil will require more care and diligence in your maintenance. Even fresh from the carton, most sergers seem to be coated with a film of oil. A commercial serger actually sits in a pan of oil when it is running.

There are two reasons for this increased use of oil:

1. Speed. A serger functions nearly twice as fast as a traditional sewing machine. This speed creates more heat. The heat breaks down the viscosity (the thickness) of the oil, which causes it to evaporate faster. Therefore the serger needs more oil.

2. Distribution of oil. The majority of overlocks have a hole on the top of the machine that the manual indicates "needs more oil." Few manuals are specific about amount. The reason you need

to put large amounts of oil in the top is that most sergers use a wick for a large part of their lubrication needs (Fig. 8.1).

This hole in the top of the serger is the uppermost part of a group of wicks. There may be as many as eight of them knotted right below the surface. These wicks feed oil to all the essential parts in the machine. The problems of a wick-fed machine are twofold:

1. Like a kerosene lantern wick, the oil in these serger wicks must travel the length of the string and fill it up before it can begin to lubricate the parts it touches.

2. The wick is exposed to the air as it makes its journey through the machine. Inside the serger the oil will simply evaporate.

What the manual means by "add more oil" is about 20 drops in the wick area about once a month.

Most of the more common oiling holes on a machine are enclosed in other metal pieces that prevent this constant evaporation. If you put the overlock away and don't use it for three months or more, oil it and let it sit for an hour or two before you begin to sew. It takes that long for the oil to work.

You almost cannot over-oil and damage a serger. The only exception to oiling too much is if you were over-

Fig. 8.1

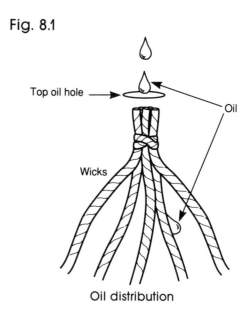

Oil distribution

zealous, going into the back or side vents and getting oil in the motor.

You **can** under-oil a serger. Listen to your machine and be aware of the changes in noise level. A serger will become louder and more clattery as it runs out of oil.

One day I was making tablecloths and napkins for a large group. I ran my serger for four straight hours, making one rolled hem after another without slowing down. Finally, the serger growled its last breath and stopped. After a ten-minute cool-off and a thorough oiling, we were off again, with no permanent damage. Don't be as careless as I was. *Listen* to your serger.

The other lubricating holes only need to be oiled every three months. They are not exposed to the air, which makes the difference in their lasting power.

Your manual has a diagram of all the spots to apply oil. Get to know this diagram. The more you use the machine, the more oil it requires. A good rule of thumb is to rock the handwheel with one hand while looking inside. Whatever moves together, oil. Proper and adequate oiling will increase the life and productivity of your machine.

Few overlock manufacturers recommend that you *don't* oil their sergers. These brands have sealed bearings. I would be wary of buying one if the machine was going to be used for sustained periods of time. However, this can be a handy feature for the infrequent sewer.

Use any standard sewing-machine oil on your serger, but nothing with additives.

Hint: Keep your Fray Check™ separate from your oil. An accidental mixup will ruin the wicks and prevent them from absorbing oil.

Cleaning Your Serger

An overlock comes with a cleaning brush, which is a subtle foretelling of things to come. Because of the serger's ability to cut or trim the fabric edges, it creates an incredible amount of fuzz.

Try to keep it fairly free of the fuzz, but you don't have to be a fanatic. Fuzz does absorb oil, and that is a real issue with these machines because of their need for oil. If allowed to accumulate, fuzz can clump and prevent your machine from operating. Clean your serger at the end of each project or more often if the fabric calls for it.

It is difficult, if not impossible, to keep your serger immaculate, but still use your brush often and liberally. If the fuzz seems to stick, dip the brush in rubbing alcohol to cut through the oil and residue. This will strip away the oil; you must replace that oil immediately.

Due to the speed at which a serger moves, the flow of thread through the tension mechanism can build up excess fuzz, dye, and surface finishing agents. The specific area to clean is between the separating disks. Loosen the tension mechanism by turning it to zero (left, counterclockwise). Dip a soft cotton cloth in rubbing alcohol and slide it between the separating plates to remove thread residue.

I recommend using caution with canned air products. Most contain freon, which is extremely cold. Instead, I use a warm hair dryer to clean my machine. I find the warmth helps cut through and thin the oil. Also, the intensity of the canned air stream has a tendency to push the threads around so violently, they dislodge from the proper thread carriers.

Prolonging the Life of Your Cutting Blades

I have a ten-year-old serger. It has been used and abused in my classroom by all my students for the last four years. This serger has probably overlocked the edges of five to ten garments per week for most of its life. If it were a car, it would have 500,000 miles on it. Yet this machine has only had three blades since it was new. One of those was wrecked by cutting 4-mil plastic to make four paint aprons. I believe the blades have had such excellent endurance because I clean and lubricate the blades every time I do the rest of the machine.

Fig. 8.2

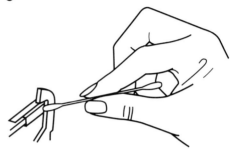

Cleaning the cutting blade

Overlocks with a blade that hangs from the top are usually designed to swing the blade up and out of the way. Locks with a cutter that comes from the bottom can also be moved away from the fixed cutter, but often it requires loosening a screw, so read your manual.

Use a cotton swab dipped in rubbing alcohol to clean the surfaces of the cutters (Fig. 8.2). After the blades are clean and dry, apply a thin film of oil on the fixed cutter, using the other end of the swab.

Removing Burrs

The most common and serious problem in an overlock can be traced to one thing—BURRS. Even the smallest nick or rough spot can wreak havoc with your stitches. Many of the so-called

Fig. 8.3

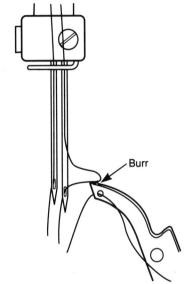

The most common overlock problem is
thread catching on a looper burr

Fig. 8.4

Remove burrs with crocus cloth folded
over screwdriver blade

chain if they catch on a burr and jerk
the thread.

Be sure to check the stitch finger,
as well as the bottom of the foot. The
constant chaining off will cause grooves
where the feed dogs scuff against the
foot, and the ridges can cause jerky
movements when the fabric slides
through.

The best way to remove burrs is to
use crocus cloth (Fig. 8.4). Crocus cloth
is located near the sandpaper in hardware stores. It is not truly sand paper,
but a super-fine buffing compound impregnated on denim.

To remove burrs on loopers and
the stitch finger, use a quarter of a sheet
of crocus cloth folded over the blade
of a small screwdriver. Stroke back and
forth evenly without hard pressure. To
smooth the bottom of the foot, put the
crocus cloth on a table, compound up.
Rotate the foot, pressing it lightly against
the crocus cloth.

tension problems of an overlock are the
result of burrs. When you clean your
machine, check thoroughly for rough
spots on the throat plate, bottom and
finger of the foot, and both loopers
(Fig. 8.3).

When a needle breaks on an overlock, it is almost guaranteed that it hit
another piece of metal. These collisions
usually cause a burr, so check carefully
after a break. The thread in the loopers
cannot slide back and forth to form the

9

THREAD: FUNCTIONAL AND DECORATIVE

The serger has been a boon to the home sewer who wants to continue sewing but has strict time limitations. A serger uses more thread than a traditional machine, so it's technically more expensive, but in today's fast-paced world we need to put value on our time. This increased use of thread is offset by the hours of time saved, as well as the improvement of the final product.

Quality and Packaging

I believe using good thread is a necessity. The influx of cheap thread sold especially for sergers is sometimes exactly that—cheap thread. *Cheap* is not always a bargain. Poor-quality thread will cause breakage, skipped stitches, and tension problems.

The characteristics of quality thread are:

Fig. 9.1

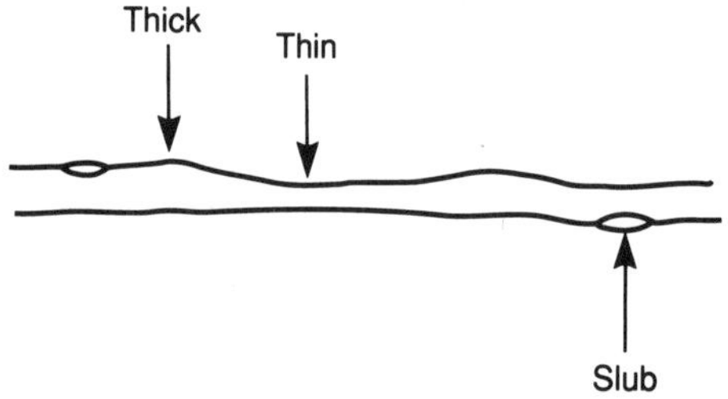

Irregular thread

Fig. 9.2

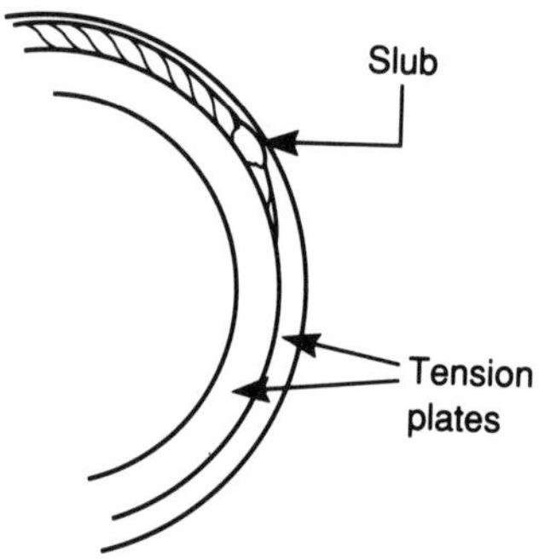

Thread slubs will pull thread out of tension

Uniformity—Uniform thread is smooth and even. If it has slubs, they are not hard chunks, but are small (Fig. 9.1). The thickness should remain the same throughout the spool. If a big slub comes off the spool and hits the tension wrong, it will slide around the dial and pull the thread out of the separating plates instead of through it (Fig. 9.2). This is why the tension occasionally goes haywire in mid-seam.

Flexibility—Flexible thread bends easily and is not stiff. The loops on the fabric are even and soft and the overcast is not prickly.

Strength—Because of the speed of an overlock, the thread takes more abuse. If the thread is uneven or has weak spots, it will break.

Hint: Be wary of a "million" yard cone advertised for $1.99. It is generally a waste of time and money because it doesn't work well on the machine.

Check in sewing-machine stores to find a large assortment of good-quality thread. They have a vested interest in making sergers perform at their best. You will find the variety you seek and the guidance on use that will make your serging successful.

Although thread quality is not quite as important on an overlock as on a traditional machine, it cannot be completely ignored. In addition to the quality of the thread, there is another variable: the way the thread is wound onto the spool or cone. Even this seemingly minor difference can make a big change in the serger's performance.

There are two ways to wind thread onto a spool. The best way for an overlock is to use an easy-release spool (Fig. 9.3). This thread, whether on a cone or small spool, has been wound in a diamond-shaped pattern that allows it to be pulled easily from the top.

Fig. 9.3

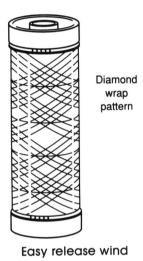

Diamond
wrap
pattern

Easy release wind

Fig. 9.4

Traditional spool

The drawback of easy-release thread is the tendency of the individual strand to slide too easily down the side of the holder. The more slippery the thread, the more frequently this happens. The thread can catch under the bottom of the spool or cone and no longer unwind. The stitches will pucker and the thread will eventually break. This can be prevented by using plastic thread nets that slip over the whole spool or cone. These are available at most dealers and can be used on any brand of serger.

The other method of winding thread is called a traditional wind (Fig. 9.4). (Dual Duty is wound on a traditional spool.) This thread is wound from the top down and then the bottom up,

one thread right next to the other. It has a small slit in the end to hold a loose thread end.

The problems caused by this type of wind are twofold: (1) As the thread unwinds from the top, it keeps catching on that little hook and can snap. (2) As the thread goes from the bottom up, it has to pull itself over the next rung of thread, yet when it winds from the top down, it can release easily. The result is 6″ of normal stitching and 6″ of too-tight stitching.

To alleviate both of these problems, overlocks come with spool caps. These are shaped like tiny frisbees or wagon wheels. You should have one for each spool holder. The caps are meant for use with traditional spools of sewing-machine thread. The spool caps sit on top of the spool and protect the ends. They also force the thread out and up, which evens out the tension.

> *Note:* Cheap thread problems sometimes show up after the garment is assembled and washed. It shrinks and puckers as it is laundered.

Colors

Only the needle thread on a seam shows on the right side of the fabric, so it is the only thread that must match if the inside is not going to be visible or on display. Therefore, you can use a blending color on large cones on the loopers and small matching color spool(s) on the needle(s).

A traditional spool of thread can be used if you really need to match a color. You will find the tension is more erratic and more difficult to adjust when you mix thread brands. Use the easy-release spools whenever possible for the best results.

Varieties and Fibers

The most common thread used in an overlock is mid-weight polyester. Polyester has the stretch and strength that are essential in the fast-moving sergers. These threads come in a variety of colors. Standard thread for sewing machines can also be used, especially the easy-release spools. Polyester also comes in finer weights for use with lingerie and other fine but stretchy fabrics.

Use cotton thread when strength is not as important as softness and flexibility. Because cotton is not as strong as polyester, work at a slower-than-normal speed. For a very fine edge on crepe de chine, try using extra-fine cotton. But sew carefully and use a reduced speed.

The manner in which a serger makes a stitch and the large eye on the loopers allow you to use a range of threads and yarns that a traditional sewing machine couldn't handle. The serger needle can be threaded with a thread of matching or contrasting color or a clear nylon monofilament. Be sure the washability of the strand is compatible with your fabric.

> *Hint:* Clear nylon thread is sometimes prickly in a seam, so experiment and adjust placement if necessary.

The maximum thickness of a strand to be put through the looper is approximately the same as fingering yarn. Here is a list of possibilities:

1. Yarn and string—Cotton, wool, linen, silk, jute, synthetics, and metallics or any combination of fibers
2. Floss—Embroidery floss, perle cotton in an assortment of weights, metallic filament, and untwisted nylon (called woolly or fuzzy) (*Beware:* nylon melts under a hot iron.)
3. Monofilament—Ribbon, very fine cord, and clear or translucent thread is made of nylon and is especially good for blind hems and the application of trims
4. Mixtures of threads

The resistance of these different overcast strands will vary greatly. It is imperative that you practice and adjust all the tensions. Often when using the unusual looper threads, you will also have to change needles and tensions. Because there are so many variables, the only way to discover the right setting is to experiment.

If any of these threads or yarns do not have enough strength to be used alone in a serger because they repeatedly break, use a strand of strong polyester or nylon thread at the same time. Just thread them both through the machine, including the tension, and handle them as one thread.

This list is only a beginning. Now that you are starting to understand how your serger works and how easy it is to adjust, you can spread your wings. Develop an eye for seeing any new string as a possibility.

Look for new ideas in yarn shops, needlework shops, craft stores, and fabric stores in the trim, ribbon, and bridal accessories departments.

Thread Guides and Supports

Most machines have some type of cone supports (one for each thread spool) made of rubber or plastic. They slide over the spool pin for use with large cones and widen the base of support, preventing the cones from wobbling around.

When you work an overlock, the telescopic extension **must** be extended to the top. If the thread guides are not aligned properly, your tension will be thrown off.

Some machines have a sliding thread bed that must be pushed from one side to the other to be in working position. For storage and travel, they slide to a safety position. If this thread bed is not in the operating position, the tension will not function properly.

Fig. 9.5

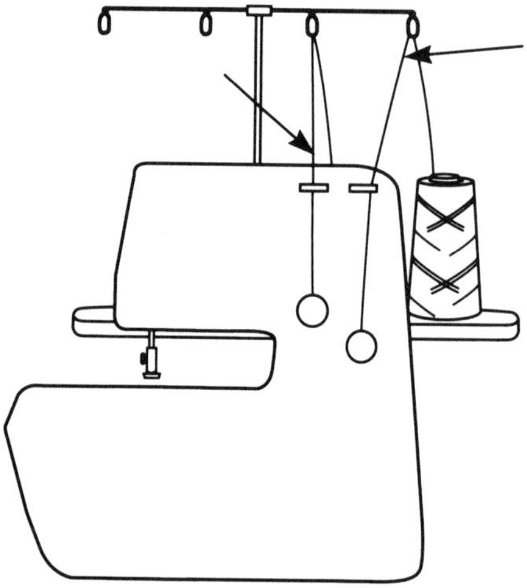

Cut looper threads at different heights

Fig. 9.6

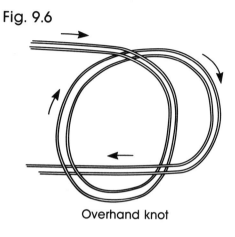

Overhand knot

Rethreading or Tying On

In Chapter 8, you learned how to thread your serger from scratch. Usually it's not necessary to rethread the entire machine. I tie the new threads onto the old threads and run them through the overlock. This makes changing your thread faster and easier.

Even when we know how to change and proof the thread, it is still a pain to redo the entire machine so here are five tips to make the change foolproof:

1. Don't try to pull a knot through the eye of a needle. It is too easy to bend the needle and will cause it to break. It is much simpler to snip the thread just above the eye of the needle and rethread the needle.

2. Cut the looper threads at different heights above the tension mechanism so you can control the timing of the knots passing through the tension (Fig. 9.5).

3. Use an overhand knot (Fig. 9.6). Hold the two ends together, make a loop, put the ends through the center of the hole, pull tight, and trim ends to 1/4".

4. Use a reduced speed.

5. Reduce the tension as the knot travels through each mechanism or the thread might pull itself out of the tension.

Thread Consumption

Each of the cones on a serger uses up different amounts of thread. The loopers use thread about three to five times as fast as the needle. If you have a chain or safety chain needle to the left, it will use the thread at about the same rate as the loopers. The reason I make this point is that you must be conscious of rotating your threads sometime about halfway through your project.

The wider the overcast seam, the faster the looper thread will be used up. A thicker looper thread or yarn will also add to the amount of thread the machine will use.

10

PROBLEMS AND MYSTERIES

Much like a traditional sewing machine, the problems on an overlock stem not from one factor but from a number of small ones. The number of threads and the different configuration of serger stitches make proper adjustment very confusing. To simplify learning how the overlock operates, to try out new methods, or to trouble-shoot a problem, *use a different color thread in each slot.* Each thread must be of the same brand and fiber content.

Stitch Formation

When the tensions are correct, the looper threads should lay evenly on the top and underside of the fabric. The shape of the threads resembles a zigzag with a slight loop along the edge.

There are two types of needle threads:

The first is part of the overcast stitch. These thread(s) hold the looper threads together. Depending on the model of the serger, there can be one or two. The thread is carried along the top of the fabric and intersects the looper each time the needle goes into the fabric. When the needle tension is correct, you will see a small loop on the underside and a single line on the top side.

The second type is the chain stitch. This thread is to the left of the edge. The top of the fabric looks very much like a traditional seam. The underside has a smooth ropelike appearance.

Tension Tips

Tension on each machine varies. The dial settings are hand-calibrated by a mechanic and can have slightly different pressure on the thread from machine to machine. These settings will also vary with thread brand and category.

> *Hint:* Make a note of each new thread or yarn you use on the worksheet in Fig. 10.1; record the tension settings that worked best, along with a sample. Then you will not need to struggle with recalculating each time you use that thread.

Instead of just twisting knobs randomly, here is a good rule of thumb when you need to adjust the tension: **Right is tight and left is loose**

Needle Tensions

The needle tensions are primarily adjusted for differences in length. The longer the stitch length, the looser the tension. The shorter the stitch length, the tighter the tension. A serger does not have an uptake or bobbin to allow more or less thread for the distance between the stitches. The farther the distance between stitches, the more thread required to cover the distance, the looser the tension should be.

Looper Tensions

The loopers are adjusted for the width of the stitch. The narrower the stitch, the tighter the tension. The wider the stitch, the looser the tension. A wide overcast edge takes more thread because of the increased distance the thread must cover. When making a very narrow edge, you don't need as much thread to go back and forth. If it is too loose, it just looks like globs.

This can be carried one step farther by realizing that the sideways distance also depends on the thickness of the fabric. When you sew on a very thin piece of fabric, the distance of the looper path is actually narrower because it doesn't have to go up over and back

Fig. 10.1 Serger sample

Date: _____

Project: _____
_____
_____

Stitch Length: _____

Needle Plate: _____

Presser Foot: _____

Presser Foot Regulator Position: _____

Tensions: Left Needle (LN)   _____
             Right Needle (RN)   _____
             Upper Looper (UP)   _____
             Lower Looper (LL)   _____

Threads: Left Needle (LN)   _____
             Right Needle (RN)   _____
             Upper Looper (UP)   _____
             Lower Looper (LL)   _____

ATTACH
STITCH
SAMPLE
HERE

down. Thick fabric uses up more thread for the opposite reason.

> *Hint:* If the tension does not seem to change when you move the dial and you are positive the thread is in the separating plates, the internal spring may be compressed. Turn the mechanism to the tightest and then the loosest settings three or four times to release the jammed spring.

If all else fails, turn all the dials to zero and start over again

Fig. 10.2

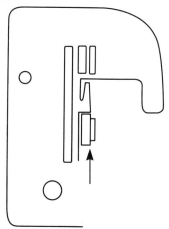

Align cutting edge with right side of stitch finger

Cutting-Blade Placement

The loops off the edge of the fabric can vary from loose and sloppy to tight and bunchy. These edges can be slightly adjusted by changing the looper tension. If adjusting the tension doesn't seem to help, the placement of the cutting blades may be the cause of the problem.

When the cutting blades are in the proper position, the area that actually cuts will be aligned in front of and even with the far right side of the stitch finger (Fig. 10.2). If the cutting blades are too far to the left, the blades will cut the fabric off narrower than the loopers can make a stitch. The tension cannot pull in a stitch narrower than the finger it creates its stitch over.

If the cutting blades are too far to the right, the blades will not cut off enough fabric and the overcast will be tight and puckered. The loopers have difficulty moving over the fabric edges and the improper motion can cause fraying.

These differences can be no more than 1/32" but can cause major problems in stitch quality.

This adjustment is the answer to the perplexing problem of large loops off the edge of knit fabrics. Even if the cutter was aligned properly for woven fabrics, it may not be correct for a knit. Knit fabrics tend to stretch and roll when they are cut. When the knit rolls, it becomes narrower than the stitch finger. The looper thread can be tightened until the thread breaks and it still will not make the loops decrease in size.

If these loops are a problem, move the cutting blades to the right until they are past the right edge of the stitch finger by 1/32″. This will cut the knit a tiny bit too wide and when the fabric snaps back, it will be the right size for the finger and the overcast edge will be correct.

Don't be afraid to learn how to move your blade. It isn't difficult.

Stabilizing a Seam

Look inside along the shoulder seam of a sweater or knit garment you have purchased. There is often a string or tape there to keep the garment from stretching out of shape.

Many overlocks are set up for you to make this type of insertion simple. You can use either a 3- or 3/4-spool setup. The additional stabilizer could be either a ball or spool of a reinforcing material. I like pearl cotton or soft ny-

Fig. 10.3

Stay tape

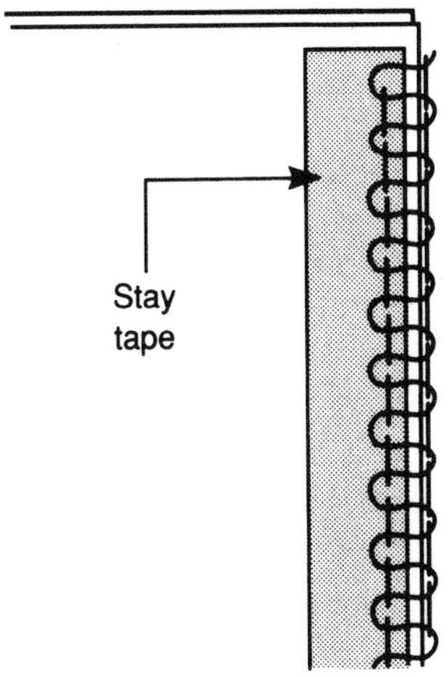

Tape used to stabilize seam

lon stabilizer tape (Fig. 10.3). Some machines have special escapements (thread carriers) to guide the stabilizer through the machine. Some feet have feed holes to hold these cords in place, so they do not get cut by the blades. The cords can be aligned so the cord is free under the thread or stitched in place.

If the cording sits free under the thread, it can also be used to gather (Fig. 10.4). The cord that lies under the overlock stitches is easily drawn up. This is especially helpful on long pieces, such as a dust ruffle with yards of fabric.

If the cording is caught in a needle seam, it will be held in place. This method offers the greatest degree of stabilization.

Fig. 10.4

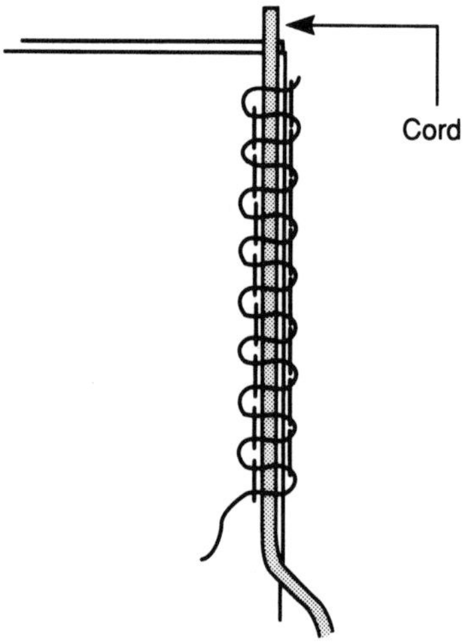

Cord

Cord used to gather seam

Fig. 10.5

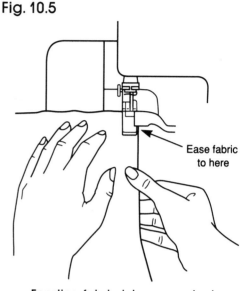

Ease fabric
to here

Feeding fabric into an overlock

Aiming the Fabric

Because the cutting and sewing element of an overlock form a squared L shape instead of a single line as a traditional machine makes, the manner in which you feed the fabric is very different from a traditional sewing machine.

The correct method for aiming the fabric is to concentrate on feeding it to the front of the foot, instead of pivoting the fabric.

The difference of feeding shows up most when you are overcasting the edges of fabric that has already been

cut out. If you tug the fabric to the right going around a curve, you will discover that the overcast is not covering the entire edge. Occasionally it will even completely miss the fabric. Going in the opposite direction will cut off more than you wish.

Gently ease the fabric, using your right hand only, to the edge of the throat plate (Fig. 10.5). This approach feeds the fabric into the overlock in the straightest method.

Get your hand out from behind the machine! Pulling on the fabric is an absolute no-no. If you tug the fabric to the rear while the needle(s) are in the fabric, they will bend to the back. Because of the close proximity of the looper to the needle, any change in the placement of the needle will cause the needle to strike the looper. This breaks the needle and very often damages the looper.

When to Remove the Cutting Blades

Removing the cutting blade is recommended for doing flatlock and other decorative edges. Flatlocking is often done in the center of the garment, so most instructions tell you to remove the blade to prevent the fabric from being cut.

Removing the movable cutter is possible on all sergers. With some models it is as easy as a flip of a dial; with others it will require a screwdriver and wrench.

No matter how simple or difficult the procedure, *be careful.* Careless use of a serger with the cutting blade removed is the most common way to jam your overlock to the point of throwing the machine out of time. In my experience, this has been the number-one cause of major repairs on sergers.

The cutter trims away the edge as the fabric travels through the machine.

The loopers can then arch over the edges to form the overcast. If the fabric extends too far over the edge, the looper will catch in the fabric while the looper is traveling at high speed.

This is similar to running your car into a curb at high speed. At the very least, your front-end alignment will need to be repaired.

Sewing with the movable cutter removed should be done (if at all) at very slow speed, so you can clearly see that it is moving straight. It should also be done on straight or barely curved seams to prevent the fabric from wandering over the edge.

I recommend that you leave the movable cutter in place all the time. If you do not want to trim the edge of the fabric, feed it carefully just to the left of the throat-plate edge. If you do cut off a small amount by accident, don't feel bad. That portion would have caused a jam.

The Mysterious Break

I have repeatedly cautioned about a knot forming instead of a chain without you realizing it. This phenomenon causes what I call the mysterious break.

The serger has been sewing along

when you hear a rasping noise and then a snapping sound. Lo and behold, one of the threads has jumped out of a looper or a needle eye but remains part of the chain.

What has actually occurred is the thread has knotted above the eye of the looper or needle and caught. As the fabric is pushed forward, the strain on the thread finally causes it to break. When it snaps, it is still attached to the chain and looks as though it has escaped the eye.

The other mysteries are also related to the repetitious nature of thread breakage. Once a break occurs and you rethread the machine, it seems to break over and over. These breaks generally occur about 1 to 1 1/2″ into the seam.

Thread-breakage problems are caused by improper threading. The reason it occurs a short distance after the beginning of a seam is that it takes this distance for the pressure on the thread to finally break it. Reread the proofing section in Chapter 6, and always thread the needle *last*.

Finishing the Chain

It is not necessary to finish the end of a serged edge unless the end will be exposed after completion. After sewing off the edge, clip the chain, leaving

Fig. 10.6

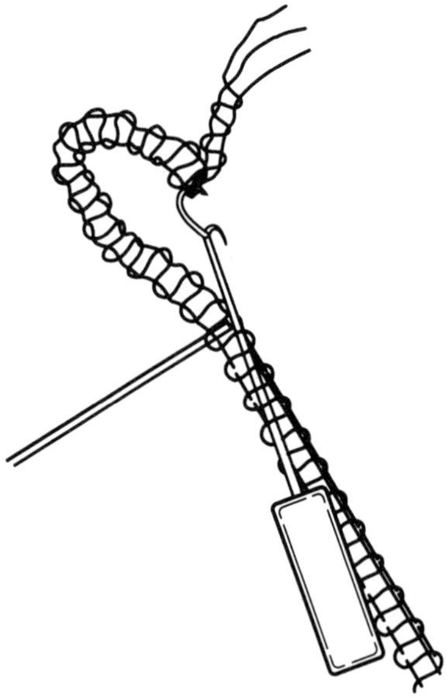

Tiny latch hook tool is used to anchor threads

at least 2″ of chained thread to prevent unravelling.

If the edge will never be caught in a cross seam, you can apply a small drop of Fray Check at the edge. Let it dry and trim away the excess.

If the seam sealant might discolor the fabric in a conspicuous place, pull the ends under the previous threads. I recommend a tiny latch hook device that is sold as a snag repair tool. The tool can be eased under the last 1/2″ of overcast. Catch the chain in the hook, *then* cut the threads off to 1/2″ and pull through (Fig. 10.6).

Never, Never, Nevers

Never #1: The movable cutter should last a long time. The fixed cutter should last ten times as long as the movable one. *But,* if you sew over one pin, you may need to replace both of them. Sewing over pins is an expensive proposition. Not only will the blades be ruined, but the entire machine could become out of time and not be able to make a stitch at all. Try using clothespins to hold fabric edges, instead of pins (Fig. 10.7).

Never #2: Never turn your handwheel against the recommended direction for your machine. Check your manual. Most manufacturers consider it important enough to show a directional arrow on the wheel. Turning the wheel in reverse will cause a knot instead of a chain, which will lead to breakage.

Never #3: Do not cut the chain off by running it through the cutter. The loose chain threads can catch in the loopers and cause a knot instead of a chain. This break doesn't happen every time, so it will make it tough to track down the problem. The time it takes to snip the thread with scissors is not worth the mess of a jam.

Fig. 10.7

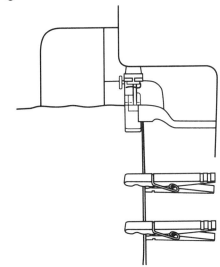

Use clothespins to hold fabric edges together

The Perfect Corner

If you got excited when you saw this heading, get ready for a jolt of reality. There is no such thing as a perfectly pivoted outside corner. The L-shaped sewing area prevents perfection. The thread must be loosened to become free of the stitch finger in order to go around a corner. The excess thread moves across the end and makes a loop. Please check ready-to-wear as an example. Most use the sew-off and sew-across method.

Fig. 10.8

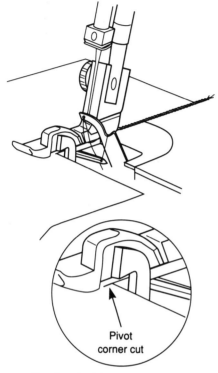

Turning inside corners

Fig. 10.9

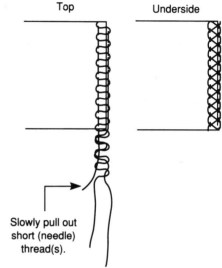

Slowly pull out short (needle) thread(s).

Removing the needle thread

the fabric to allow you to pivot the fabric. Do not try to *force it through in a straight line*. Otherwise, as you sew over the corner, you will get a pucker.

Removing Overcast Stitches

The needle threads hold an overcast edge together. If you remove these threads, the looper threads will just fall off.

To pivot an inside corner, you must watch the cutting blades as you approach a corner. When the serger cuts one slice into the corner, leave the foot and needle down and bring the new side straight down, even with the edge of the throat plate (Fig. 10.8). The cut acts like a clip on a garment and frees

You can find the needle threads in a chain by running a fingernail over the chain to straighten it out. The one or two shorter threads are the needle threads.

Grasp one thread and pull gently, sliding it along like a gather thread until it comes out (Fig. 10.9). If necessary, slide out the second needle thread.

If the thread snaps, loosen the next few needle threads on the top and resume pulling it out.

Hint: The top-side needle thread is straight and the underside is scalloped or just a small knot.

Troubleshooting is really a matter of prevention. Sergers are not more difficult to use than traditional machines. They are just different. Remember, if you do have problems, **check one thing at a time.**

PART III
KNITTING MACHINES

INTRO-
DUCTION

After discovering the joys of the sewing machine and serger, the sewing public is eager for other exciting outlets for their creativity. The newest entry into the home-arts machine market is the knitting machine.

People are using the knitting machine in exciting combinations with their other machines: knitting a matching ribbing for a knit fabric, for example, or knitting flat yardage which is cut and serged into whole sweaters or parts of garments. Others use their knitting machines for the boring parts of hand-knit sweaters, such as the backs and sleeves.

After spending time investigating this newest craze, I have decided it is almost impossible for a consumer to determine which model or type is best without having some basic background information.

The alternatives in knitting machines and knitting frames are so varied that it's easy to become overwhelmed and confused. Each type of knitting machine has strict limitations on the features it can offer and the thread weight it can handle.

The information in this section will be presented in a different way than for the sewing machine and serger sections. The focus will be on how each type of knitting machine functions and how each differs from the others.

This section does not pretend to offer the whole story on knitting machines, but it does give you the essentials and a way of understanding the differences so that you can make informed choices.

11

HOW A KNITTING MACHINE REALLY WORKS

I am not as expert on knitting machines as I am on sewing machines and sergers, but I have used my mechanical expertise to present an unbiased point of view, describing how they work from a functioning viewpoint—beyond the flurry of information and claims.

All knitting machines make a knitted stitch, not a crochet stitch or macramé knot. The knitted stitch is an interlocking row of loops that build on each other. The knitting-machine stitches are exactly like hand-knit stitches, except they are more even.

A knitting machine does the actual knitting of the yarn. You don't need to know how to knit to operate the machine. You *do* need to know how to operate the knitting machine, however, whether or not you know how to knit. In this respect, the novice or expert start at the same level.

A hand-knitter will have the advantage after learning to operate a knitting machine. Techniques such as shaping will be easier to grasp if you know how to knit by hand, and your creative ideas may develop faster with a hand-knitting background.

Types of Knitting Machines

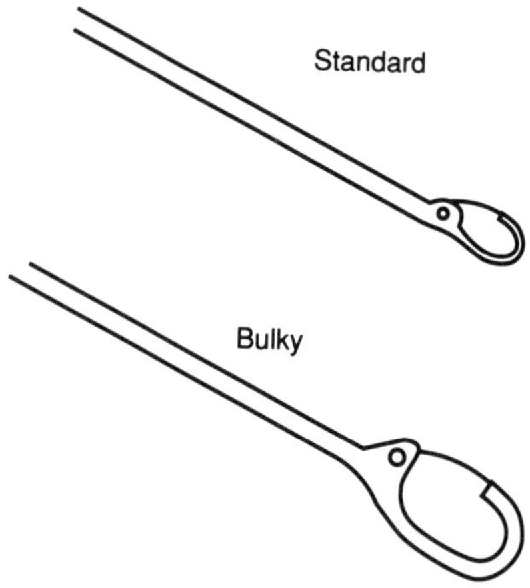

All knitting machines and knitting frames make stitches with a series of latch hooks, instead of with two standard knitting needles. These hooks are commonly referred to as needles, but I will continue to call them hooks because that is how they look and function.

There is one hook for each stitch in a row. Hooks hold the looped stitches in place. To make a new row, the carriage is pulled across the bed. The hook grabs the new yarn and pulls it through the old loop to make a new stitch.

The main difference between the two types of knitting machines is the size of the needles (hooks) and the space between them. The two basic categories, with tiny variations from brand to brand, are **standard** and **bulky.**

The standard size is the smaller of the two varieties and uses fine yarns.

Fig. 11.1

Hook sizes

The maximum thickness is the width of fingering yarn. A heavier sweater can be made by using more than one yarn at a time. The standard-size knitting machine gives a smoother, tighter look to the finished product, with a distinctly machine-knit quality.

The simplest style of knitting machine is usually referred to as a knitting *frame* instead of a "machine." The main difference is the method of adjusting the thread tension.

The bulky knitting machine uses thicker knitting yarns. The hooks are much larger and farther apart. The finished product will closely resemble a hand-knit garment.

Small yarn on a bulky machine will yield a narrow, knitted piece. The large

Fig. 11.2

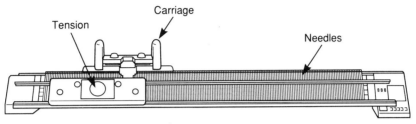

Single-bed knitting machine

needles remain the same distance apart, and the number of stitches per row is limited to the number of hooks. The finished product will be very loose and flimsy.

A Knitting Machine's Basic Parts

The basic parts of a knitting machine are:

1. Hooks—These small latch hooks function as the knitting needle and are often referred to as needles. For the sake of clarity, I will continue to call them *hooks*. The hooks come in two basic sizes—standard and bulky (Fig. 11.1).
2. Bed—The bed is a long flat surface with grooves to hold the hooks (Fig. 11.2).
3. Carriage—The carriage slides across the bed and carries the yarn

Fig. 11.3

Transfer tools

through the hooks to form new stitches.
4. Tension—The tension dial or key plates regulate the amount of pull on the thread.
5. Transfer tools—These prongs with handles can have a latch hook at the end or one or more rounded end(s), each with an eye (Fig. 11.3).

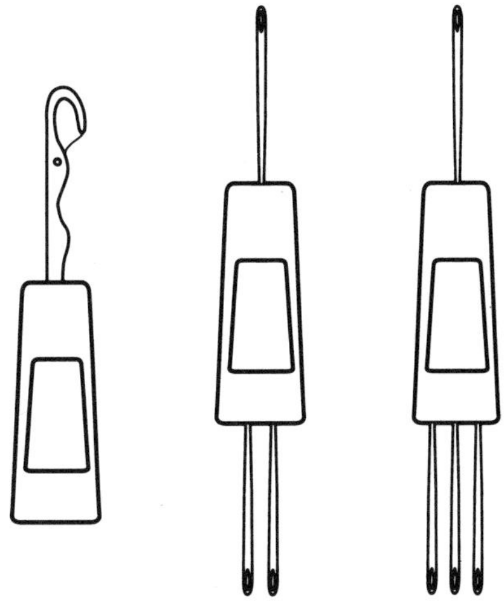

6. Weights—The weights hang from the knitting and hold the loops in the hooks. There are both weights that hang from the whole knitted piece and small ones that hang from an exact area that needs additional hold.
7. Wax—The carriage needs wax to slide smoothly over needles.
8. Knitting machine table—Knitting machines are wide and require careful anchoring. They work best anchored to a surface made specifically for the machine.

Knitting machines have many options and accessories. Some come with the machine and some must be added on. Be aware that the options are usually not interchangeable. Only certain models and brands can accept additional parts. Check the manual carefully before you make a decision.

How to Choose the Right Machine

The question of options and choices can be complicated. To help you decide the best type of machine for you, use the worksheet in Fig. 11.4.

Fig. 11.4 Checklist for Purchasing a Knitting Machine

- What type of finished product do you prefer?
    - ☐ Hand-knit appearance
    - ☐ Fine, soft look of ready-to-wear
- What categories of yarn will you use most (weight and variety)?
    - ☐ Very fine, almost thread weight
    - ☐ Mohair or other fuzzy types
    - ☐ Bulky wools, including handspun
    - ☐ Varying thickness, slubs, and/or loops
- What design options do you want?
    - ☐ Variety of patterns
    - ☐ Lacework
    - ☐ Color changes—both Fair Isle and intarsia
    - ☐ Ribbing—by hand or by machine
- What kind of automation do you want?
    - ☐ Punchcard
    - ☐ Electronic
    - ☐ Shaping
- Do you want weights? ☐

- What size machine would be best?
    - ☐ Standard (pluses and minuses)
    - ☐ Bulky (pluses and minuses)
    - ☐ Interchangeable
- How much knitting do you plan to do?
    - ☐ How much time are you willing to devote to learning machine operation?
    - ☐ Will the machine be cost-effective?
    - ☐ Will you use the machine only as a hobby?
- Where should you purchase the machine? *
    - ☐ What are the dealer's lesson policies?
        - ☐ number
        - ☐ length
        - ☐ time limit
        - ☐ repeat
    - ☐ Is instructor expertise available?
    - ☐ Is the dealer reliable?
    - ☐ What is the repair procedure?

* This would be my number-one consideration, once I made the decision to buy.

12

ESSENTIALS AND OPTIONS

The more basic the kitting machine, the fewer add-on features the machine is capable of handling. The fancier the machine, the more options that can be added. This chapter helps you sort out your options so that you can make an informed purchase.

Stitch Designs

There are two variables used to create different designs: (1) fancy stitch pattern, and (2) lacework.

In a fancy stitch pattern, the design is made according to how the small variations in the yarn intertwine and cross over. These patterns will resemble stripes, squares, stars, and pleats worked right into the yarn (Fig. 12.1). In lacework, small openings are added to the patterns to give the look of lace (Fig. 12.2).

Fig. 12.1

Cable pattern

Fig. 12.3

Intarsia

Fig. 12.2

Lacework

Fig. 12.4

Fair Isle pattern

Changing Designs by Changing Colors

Different types of designs can be made simply by changing the color of the yarn.

▶ Jacquard—A fine yarn with the yarns on the back evenly flecked. The color is pulled to the front as the stitch is made. Up to four colors at a time may be used.

▶ Intarsia—Large blocks of color are knitted with a single strand of each color that is twisted in and out when the colors intersect and is then picked up in the next row (Fig. 12.3). This leaves a single layer of yarn. In an intarsia design, both the front and back of the garment look the same.

▶ Fair Isle—The different color yarns are carried along the back and brought to the front when that color is desired (Fig. 12.4). The back has a series of long carry-over threads.

Automated Features

Automated options range from punchcards and computerization of patterning, to increased color carriers for more colorful patterns, to additional beds for ribbing or patterns and motorized carriage for faster output.

The automated punch card or computerized systems determine which needle is engaged and how the pattern is formed. To achieve a uniform pattern, each row must be knitted in exactly the right order. These automated systems make the selections even and simple. Automated options make the knitting faster and simpler, but they do not do the shaping.

To do some stitch patterns, you need a double-bed machine. The beds are aligned with the needles meeting in the center at right angles (Fig. 12.5). A pair of interlocking carriages make both beds function as one for fancy work. The second bed is needed to make ribbing and lacework. Some machines require additional attachments to do ribbing.

The Tension Dial

Increasing or decreasing the tension determines the size of the stitches. A standard knitting machine has a tension dial or dials similar to a sewing machine. Adjusting the dial causes the separating plates to press against the yarn. This adjusts the drag on the yarn

Fig. 12.5

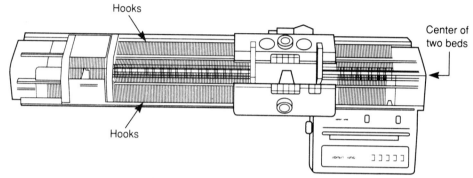

Double-bed knitting machine

and makes the knitted piece tighter or looser.

Knitting frames require the change of a key plate. This plate alters how far the thread is stretched as it travels over a row. They have three to five different plates for their range of tension.

Basic Operations

Shaping

Shaping is a method of creating the outline of a completed piece. Making the knitted piece larger is called *increasing* or *casting on*. Making the garment smaller is called *decreasing* or *casting off*.

Casting on is done to start knitting by putting the first row of loops on blank hooks or to add on large sections to the edges. This is done by hand by running thread through the hooks. Increasing is adding a few stitches into the body of the piece.

Casting off is done when the garment is completed to finish the edge and make it secure from raveling, or when an opening is needed in the center of a piece. Decreasing is knitting a few stitches together to make the row of stitches narrower.

Increasing and Decreasing

Increase and decrease must still be done by hand. The method depends on how acute a decrease or increase you need.

1. The first method uses a transfer tool with one, two, or three tines with

a hole in the end of each. The tine slips into a knitted loop, lifts the stitch(es) off the hook, and eases it onto the stitch next to it. Then as the carriage moves across, the two stitches on one hook are knitted as one and the row is decreased by the number of stitches that have been moved.

2. The second method is used when you need a rapid decrease, such as the bottom of an armhole. A tool is used with a single prong with a latch hook on the end. The knit loop is put onto the tool. The next loop is put in the latch hook and pulled through the first loop. One at a time, you decrease (chain off) the number of stitches needed for the shape of the garment.

Assembly

The most common way to sew together a knitted piece is with a large hand sewing needle and a single strand of yarn. An alternative method uses the knitting machine to join two pieces. Leave the edge to be joined on the hooks and hang the additional portion of the garment you want added onto the same hooks. A good example would be shoulder seams. The pieces are joined when you run the carriage across.

Purists will probably get huffy, but I prefer using a serger. Don't forget to loosen your pressure regulator to prevent ruffled edges. If you have it, use a differential feed. This is an excellent option for the knitter with limited time who still wants to make creative garments or crafts.

Weights

Some models need weights to keep the stitches in the hooks as the carriage slides over the yarn. The weights are attached to the knitted piece hanging down, to keep the loose loops taut in the channels and to prevent the piece from lifting up as you work.

The weights are a long strip with notches for attaching a string along the entire bottom of the garment (Fig. 12.6). This type of weight is a necessity for frame knitters. Without a constant tug on the yarn, it would jump out of the hooks and drop stitches.

Having to manipulate the yarn around the hook any more than necessary can mean an increase in the number of skipped stitches. This would include creating cables, decreases, and other fancy patterns. Adding a small spot weight will improve the quality of the stitch. These weights have small hooks or claws that attach to the sweater body or yardage (Fig. 12.7).

The knitting frame (bulky size) requires the constant use of weights, whereas the most sophisticated stan-

Fig. 12.6

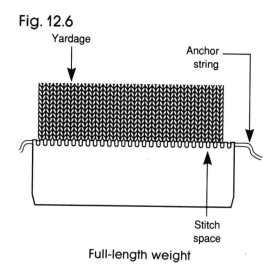

Yardage

Anchor string

Stitch space

Full-length weight

dard-size machines claim not to need weights at all. Nevertheless, all machines will benefit from at least a limited use of weights to make the knitted piece smoother and to skip resistance.

Gauging Device

The gauge refers to the number of rows in one direction and the number of stitches in the other, both calculated according to the number of each in a 1″ square.

These numbers are used to chart a pattern or to decide whether a pattern will come out according to size. Knitting machines have special measuring devices to simplify this process.

Fig. 12.7

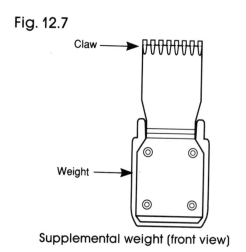

Claw

Weight

Supplemental weight (front view)

Knitting Machine Tables

Knitting machines are large and cumbersome. The motion of the carriage means the machine must be clamped to whatever it sits on. Once you start a project, you cannot move it without losing stitches.

All these details mean the best place for a knitting machine is on its own table. Fortunately, there are several varieties. Check with your dealer.

PARTING THOUGHTS

Your machines can become your good friends if you will take time to think about how to work them, rather than fighting them. Think about what you want to accomplish before beginning to sew. The reasoning process is not difficult, but it does take some practice. The time spent can save frustration and money.

Most of all, remember that you are always aiming for the look of the entire garment or craft, not for the perfect section. In other words, the quest for the perfect seam may not be good for the whole of the garment.

Besides, anyone who is inside your garment is definitely not looking at your seams!

So please read and reread this information, until it becomes a natural part of your sewing process. It can help to make enjoyable sewing and beautiful creations the best new habit you develop this year.

APPENDIX

HOW TO BUY A SEWING MACHINE, OVERLOCK, OR KNITTING MACHINE

At some pont in the life of everyone who sews, the question arises: What is the best machine to buy? The answer is, there is no "best" machine. Each person's skills, requirements, and imagination make that answer unique. There are many factors to consider before you will be able to come up with *your* best answer.

1. What dealerships and repair shops are available in your area?
2. Is the dealer capable of teaching and servicing?
3. Do you want a machine you can add attachments to?
4. What do you expect from your machine?
5. Will you be sewing or knitting primarily garments or crafts?
6. Will you be sewing and knitting frequently or seldom?
7. What kinds of fabrics or yarn will you be using most? Do you intend to expand your range?
8. What options or features are you willing to give up to meet your budget restraints?
9. Do you want to be able to make decorative stitches and patterns?
10. Will you be sewing and knitting for children?

All these answers make a difference in your decision, but you can make that choice more successfully by following a few guidelines.

Above all, *never* buy the first machine you see, no matter how swell the dealer tells you it is. When you start looking for machines, look around. Make a list of possible brands and stores and go to a minimum of three before choosing. No exceptions! If you are pressured or told that a certain deal is available only that day, they are trying too hard to sell.

The Demo

It is important to go through the demonstration the salesperson will give you. When he or she is finished, ask if you may try the machine yourself. Ask if lessons are included in the purchase price, or if they are extra. How many are there? How long do they last? Will you have some samples to take home? Will you be able to participate in the lessons or just watch? You don't want a strictly demonstration lesson; it must be hands-on to learn correctly.

If possible, meet the person who will give the lessons. Is he or she a qualified and knowledgeable teacher who you would be comfortable learning from?

Ask about parts and the availability of attachments. Are they kept in stock or must they be ordered? Are they available nationwide (if you move)?

Be aware that many of the labor guarantees are linked to the store where you purchase the machine and not to the manufacturer. The parts are warrantied, but as a general rule, the biggest expense is labor: it can be three times as costly! Ask to see the Labor Warranty. It must be available for you to look at. (There will be exclusions about electrical parts, but that's standard.)

When shopping for a sewing machine or serger, take a selection of fabrics with you to every store for each machine you try. Let the person give you guidance on stitch selection and thread, but *do not* let that person do all the sewing.

One fabric you should test is a long piece of medium-weight cotton, just to feel how evenly and smoothly it feeds through the machine. Let the feed dogs move the fabric both forward and in reverse for a few inches without you holding onto the fabric. A machine should sew straight, without veering to one side or the other. (Sewing in reverse will never work as well as forward because of the way a machine functions, but the difference should not be drastic.)

Another test should be to see how well the machine handles a thick or dense piece. You want to sew a seam to see how the machine travels up and over thick fabric. All machines have a limit to how much fabric can be fed through, but you need to know the possibilities of each machine and which one balks first.

Work on a knit, preferably tricot, to see if it skips and slides. You also want to try a piece of very thin material to see if the feed dogs hold it firmly enough as it flows through the machine. Remember, the test of a good machine is how it sews finer fabrics. This test should show the precision and care with which the machine moves this fabric, as problems show up most on fine, easily damaged material.

Last, bring a piece of fabric that has always given you problems. Don't let the salesperson talk you into just using the stiff, white fabric-on-a-roll that always makes stitches look good.

Wind a bobbin yourself, following the manufacturer's directions. Then check the following: Was it easy to set up? How does the bobbin look? Is it evenly filled across? Is the thread firmly against the bobbin with no loose spots?

> *Note:* Do not wind through the eye of the needle no matter what anyone tells you. The slubs on threads make for inconsistencies in bobbin winding that can cause tension problems.

Sewing Machine Features and Options

Plastic Versus Metal

Be aware of salespeople who tell you that metal machines are better because any plastic is bad. That's not necessarily true. Just as metal varies in quality (look at the range in pans), there are different qualities of plastic, from bulletproof shields to cheap combs whose teeth fall out at first use. Look into the kind of plastic they're talking about and don't assume that all metal machines are automatically stronger.

Stitch Formation

You may hear the terms "rotary" and "oscillator". These refer to how the machine forms the stitch. "Rotary" means the race moves around in one continuous circle. "Oscillator" means a movement back and forth in semicircles. There are pros and cons to both. This feature should not influence you on a machine's suitability for you.

You also will be confronted by options such as whether to buy a computerized machine. Keep in mind that a sewing machine is meant to sew your clothing together. The manner in which the stitches are selected (this is the only part that is computerized) is not nearly as important as the quality of the stitches themselves. The machine still has to make its stitch; it still has to sew a seam. Don't become so mesmerized by all the features that you stop looking at stitch quality.

When you're looking at machines, be aware of oversimplified features. You don't want to be locked into not being able to choose alternatives or override a computer. For example, you know that not every buttonhole will wind up on a flat surface. If you have a machine so overautomated that you cannot deal with variables, you have lost a good deal of control.

Tension

One of the biggest arguments you will hear is the "my tension is better than yours" syndrome. The better machines use heavier springs, so the tension does stay in adjustment. Many manufacturers use terms such as "universal" or "automatic," but *all* machines must have some kind of tension-adjustment feature. Some have better locations or adjustment systems, but which one actually functions best is usually a matter of individual preference. Check how the stitch is balanced on your own fabric samples to judge which machine's tension system you prefer.

Stitches

When you look at the number of utility and decorative stitches offered, make sure they will be useful to you. If you have no children, never sew crafts, and rarely use knits, you probably don't need all the options now available in many machines.

It is probably important to have some kind of reverse-cycle stretch stitches. They are especially useful as reinforcement stitches because they won't rip out in high-stress areas. Some of these stitches also sew durable seams on knits.

If you plan to do a lot of mending, you might also be sure the machine you purchase features a "serpentine" or "running" stitch, which looks like a broken zigzag. It also is wonderful as an overcast stitch for facings and single layers if you don't own an overlock or serger.

Free Arm

The free arm is another option that is handy, but it does have limited uses. It takes some effort and concentration to change your method of sewing if you're used to a flat bed machine. Know that you want to change before you decide this is a feature you can't live without. On the positive side, the free arm makes hemming pants and sewing cuffs on any tubular form much easier. On the bad side, with rare exception, your current sewing cabinet cannot accommodate a free arm.

As well, make sure that the arm with or without an extension is wide enough to comfortably feed the fabric through. Sometimes it is uncomfortable to sew on the limited space of a free arm.

Bells and Whistles

Needle position aids in accurate, straight stitching lines, especially on edge-stitching and 1/4″ seams. When you can move the needle instead of the fabric, you usually can keep the needle from falling off the edge and making wavy stitch lines by keeping more of the fabric in contact with the feed dogs. Without adjustable needle position, it is often impossible to properly adjust (line up) attachments such as a rolled hem foot.

Many brands have feed dogs that drop; in others, they can't. There are some disadvantages to their not being able to drop, but these machines usually come with a piece that can be attached to the throat plate to cover the feed dogs—for example, for darning or outline quilting, or whenever you move the fabric horizontally as well as vertically.

Pressure regulators were invented to keep enough pressure between fabric and feed dogs for a smooth feed. Today, most machines are spring-loaded and the use of interchangeable feet makes this feature unnecessary.

If you look at a machine whose salespeople promise the look of an overlock or serger with certain overcast stitches, know that the two are completely different machines and can never make stitches that look identical. A serger forms its stitch without a bobbin. The thread comes directly off the spool through dials, and the machine forms its stitch with loopers that require very light tension or resistance on the thread to perform smoothly. The serger is very quick and offers variables not available with a home machine, no matter what salespeople may tell you.

If you are primarily interested in constructing garments, you might consider *not* buying a top-of-the-line sewing machine, and buy a serger as well.

Attachments

When you look for attachments, make sure that nothing on the machine is so exclusive to it that you can't use alternate attachments such as presser feet. For instance, some machines are available that cannot take anything *but* the foot system that goes with them. Look for a machine with a standard shank that will accept interchangeable attachments. This will allow you versatility as new items come on the market. If the feet are not interchangeable, ask if there is an adaptor available so you might update and expand the system as desired. If you can use only the feet that come with the machine, they had better be the only ones you'll ever want and they had better be well designed because you will be stuck.

Comfort

While testing the various fabrics on each machine, make some mental notes on how the machine feels to you. Does it fit you? Is the height proper? Are the dials easy to see, read, and use? Is the foot pedal comfortable and easy to control? Is it portable in case you want to use it away from home? Does it have a handle or carrying case? How much does it weigh with and without the case?

Note: Several manufacturers offer a dual-voltage option if you plan to use their machine outside the United States, or with DC current.

It is also important to check the amount of control you will be able to achieve over both the needle's penetrating power and the speed of the foot pedal or control. You don't want a machine that only offers jack-rabbit starts or jerky sewing. It should suit your own style of sewing.

Cost

Reasons for the differences in the cost of machines are not always obvious. More expensive machines use higher-quality materials and surfaces, so all pieces are better tooled. Everything is more durable and runs more smoothly. Smoother separating plates on sewing machines and sergers, for example, while not visible to the naked eye perhaps, won't catch the little thread fibers and create tension problems down the line.

Although quality products will cost more, don't always go for price alone. Many times the most expensive machine is not the best for you! It may have too many features you'll never use, and the best deal is not always the cheapest price. The difference in service, lessons, and overall customer relations can make or break a sale.

Last, But Not Least

Ask to see the owner's manual. Take time to read a portion of it. Is it well written and complete? Are the illustrations sensible and clear? Check the section on making buttonholes. This usually is the most complicated process on machines and often the most confusing in the instructions. If it makes sense, that's a good indication of a decent manual that will help you through the years.

You might also check you local Better Business Bureau for store background if you're not sure you are dealing with an established, franchised dealer. Buy only from a licensed representative of the manufacturer. Above all, make sure that wherever you buy the best machine for you the store has the capacity for service and repair.

Be wary of offers that seem too good to be true. They are!

INDEX